P9-ARK-872

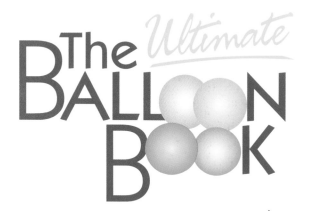

The Ultimate BALLOON BOOK

The *Ultimate* BALLOON BOOK

46 Projects to Blow Up, Bend & Twist

SHAR LEVINE & MICHAEL OUCHI

STERLING PUBLISHING CO., INC. NEW YORK

ACKNOWLEDGMENTS

Our thanks to the wonderful models who volunteered their
time on a hot summer's day

Photography by Jeff Connery
Illustrations by Jackie Aher,
assisted by Mo Moussa
Book design by Chris Swirnoff

Library of Congress Cataloging-in-Publication Data
Levine, Shar, 1953–
The ultimate balloon book: 46 projects to blow up,
bend & twist /Shar Levine and Michael Ouchi.
p. cm.
Includes index.
ISBN 0-8069-2959-6
1. Balloon sculpture. I. Ouchi, Michael. II. Title.
TT926.L48   2000
745.594—dc21   00-061899
5 7 9 10 8 6
Published by Sterling Publishing Company, Inc.
387 Park Avenue South, New York, N.Y. 10016
© 2001 by Shar Levine and Michael Ouchi
Distributed in Canada by Sterling Publishing
$^{c}/_{o}$ Canadian Manda Group, One Atlantic Avenue, Suite 105
Toronto, Ontario, Canada M6K 3E7
Distributed in Great Britain and Europe by Chris Lloyd at Orca Book Services
Stanley House, Fleets Lane, Poole BH15 3AJ England
Distributed in Australia by Capricorn Link (Australia) Pty Ltd.
P.O. Box 704, Windsor, NSW 2756, Australia
Printed in China
All rights reserved

Sterling ISBN 0-8069-2959-6

DEDICATION

For Josh and the first graduating class at West Point Grey Academy, Vancouver, BC, Canada. Many thanks to the teachers, administration, and support staff for their great work over the last 5 years.—SL

For my wife, Tracy, who has always been there for me no matter what I do. To our son, Maxwell, who reminds me on a daily basis what is truly important.—MO

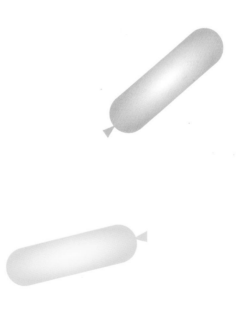

Contents

Introduction

It's hard to believe that with a few simple twists and turns a long, straight balloon can evolve into a dinosaur, a flower, a musical instrument, or even a hair ornament. Making a sculpture is quite easy when you break it down into simple steps. As you fold, twist, and turn the balloons, a form soon begins to appear. Balloon creations are symmetrical—whatever you do on one side of the balloon, you will probably be doing on the other.

Like most skills, it will take time and practice to become a balloon artist. There will be lots of frustration along the way and you will probably make more than your fair share of mutant creatures. But in the end you will be able to whip off a complicated animal at the drop of a hat. The important thing is to have fun as you learn.

So grab a bag of balloons and let's get started!

Chapter 1: Materials

There's not a lot you need to make amazing balloon creations. Basically, there's balloons and, well, balloons. There are a few items that will make balloon blowing easier and add personality to your creations. Here are the essentials:

- Balloons
  Animal entertainer or 260 balloons
  Bee body or 321 balloons*
  Airship or 350 specialty balloons*

- Round balloons* (12-, 14-, and 16-inch plain colored)
- Balloon hand pump (optional)
- Scissors
- Pin
- Sharpie® or other felt marker with non-alcohol ink
- Adult helper
- Masking tape

*NOTE: The names of some balloons vary depending on the manufacturer and the size of the balloon.

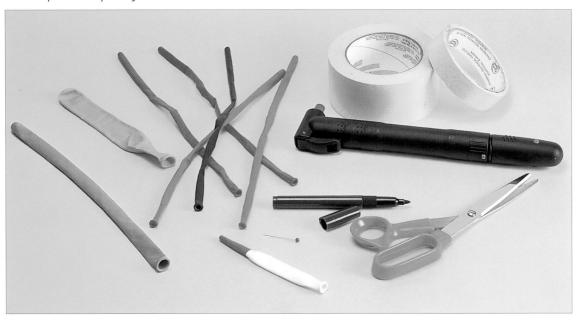

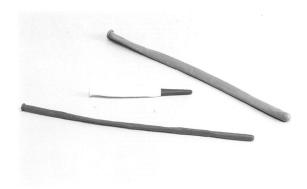

Balloons come in all shapes and sizes. Some are used as decoration for parties and celebrations. Others are meant for making creations. In this book we'll be exploring the kinds that can be folded and twisted into interesting shapes.

TYPES OF BALLOON

Long skinny balloons are usually identified by a three-digit number (for example: 260). The first digit indicates the diameter (in inches) of a fully inflated balloon. The following two digits refer to the length (also in inches) of the fully inflated balloon. So, our 260 balloon example will inflate up to 2 inches wide and 60 inches long. Sometimes, however, you can end up with a large variation of sizes when you use the same type of balloon. Even within the same package you'll find that different colors inflate to different sizes.

WHERE TO PURCHASE BALLOONS

In order to make the projects in this book, you'll need to use balloons especially made for twisting and turning. These balloons can be ordered over the Internet or purchased in party and novelty stores. You get what you pay for. In general, the less expen-sive the balloon, the more fragile the balloon will be.

HOW A BALLOON IS MADE

Manufacturers must make sure that their balloons have an even thickness, no holes, and no "funny taste." This isn't easy to do. Sophisticated science and advanced chemistry are involved in the actual making of a balloon. The process starts with a substance called "latex," which is the sap from a special kind of rubber tree found in places like Malaysia. The latex is cured and then mixed with various chemicals, oil, water, and colorings. The colored latex is poured into large tanks. A balloon-shaped mold is dipped into a special "coagulant," or liquid mixture, and then dried. This coagulant will cause the latex to stick to the mold. The mold is then dipped into the latex. Rotating brushes push up some of the latex to create the mouth, or rolled end, of a balloon. As the mold continues down the production line, it is rinsed in hot water and then baked at a low temperature for about 20 minutes. The finished balloon is pulled off the mold and bagged.

STORING BALLOONS

Fold your balloons into a sealable plastic bag and place this bag into an insulated lunch container. If you have room in your refrigerator, you can also place the bag in a safe spot. This keeps the balloons cold, dry, and away from the light.

Chapter 2: Safety Tips

Before you start learning the basic techniques in making your creations, you should be aware of some general safety and handling tips about balloons.

WORKING WITH BALLOONS

Balloons break. Even the most expert balloonist breaks an occasional balloon while twisting it to make a figure. Don't be afraid to give the balloons a good twist. But be careful when blowing up balloons. Cup the palm of your hand over the top of the balloon as you blow into it. That way, if the balloon pops, your eyes are protected from any flying pieces that may snap back at you. When you are twisting the balloon, you should also keep it far away from your face to avoid any similar accidents.

Also, this may seem obvious, but you'll probably want to have short fingernails if you are going to make these creations. Use a nail file to round off rough edges of your nails. Some professionals use a squirt of hand cream to soften their hands before twisting balloons. Other balloon artists use a dab of talcum powder on the outside of their balloons. The theory behind the powder it that it makes it easier to perform some of the balloon twists. But talcum can also make it harder to perform certain twists because you will not be able to get a good grip on the balloons. You don't need to dust your creations with powder. It will take some time, but soon you will be able to twist and turn your way to a perfect sculpture.

Sometimes you may find it difficult to hold more than one balloon at a time. Ask a friend to hold one end of the balloon while you twist and turn the other balloons.

Finally, remember that practice makes perfect. It's difficult to be able to twist balloons to be exactly the same size. The more you work at the creations, the easier it will be to make the designs.

DO'S AND DON'TS

Here are some other simple rules to follow in order to ensure that your balloon-making experience is safe and fun:

● Store your balloons in a cool, dry place away from the sun. They will last longer.
● Do not chew on balloons or place balloons in your mouth!

- Do not blow into a balloon that another person has already been blowing. You can pick up some nasty germs that way.
- When you are twisting a balloon, keep the balloon far away from your face to avoid any accidents.
- When you are doing the balloon-puff technique, do not suck on the balloon to create the puff. You can choke on the balloon.
- Do not use helium to inflate your balloons.
- Do not put any special powders or other materials inside the balloons.
- Do not use regular round balloons to make your creations. These balloons are not meant for twisting and turning.
- Do not use alcohol-based felt markers to draw on your balloons. These markers will eat through the balloon.
- Make sure you pick up all burst balloon pieces. Small children and animals might swallow them.
- Tell an adult immediately if you have hurt yourself or a friend in any way!

Chapter 3: Basic Techniques

Here are some simple terms you need to know before you begin folding balloons.

Bubble: The inflated portion of a balloon formed between two twists.

Mouth: The part of the balloon you put your lips over to blow up the balloon.

Tail: The rounded end or tip of the balloon.

Joint: The thin piece of latex created from a twist.

Twist: The turning and rotating of a balloon that will form a bubble and a joint.

Balloon puff: A special bubble formed in the tail of a blown balloon.

INFLATING A BALLOON

Professional balloonists make it look so simple to blow up balloons. It is easy for them, but it's going to take some practice for it to become that easy for you. There are a number of tricks to blowing up a long, thin balloon.

Using Your Breath

Hold the ends of the balloon and give it a quick stretch to loosen it up. Use the thumb and index finger of one hand to squeeze the

balloon about 1 inch (2.5 cm) from the opening. With your other hand hold the mouth of the balloon between your lips and blow up just the 1 inch (2.5 cm) section of balloon. As you continue to blow, pull the balloon away from you with the hand squeezing the balloon. When you have a small bubble of air, stop there and take a deep breath. Now blow into the balloon as you slowly pull your fingers down the balloon. This stretches the balloon and makes it easier for you to inflate it.

Do not fill your cheeks with air and make a face that looks like a puffer fish! You don't want to blow with your cheeks! Instead, blow air from your diaphragm. Put your hand just about a couple of inches above your navel. Your diaphragm is inside there.

Depending on the thickness and length of the balloon, it may take several breaths to fully fill the balloon. Do not try to blow the entire balloon up with one breath! Always leave at least an inch or two at the tail or tip of the balloon. This gives the air in the balloon somewhere to go to when you are pushing and twisting it.

Using a Pump

Even professional balloon artists get winded after blowing balloons all day. A simple air pump can come to the rescue.

Place the open end of the balloon over the mouth of the pump. Hold the balloon firmly in place with one hand and use your other hand to pull the plunger back. Push the plunger back and forth to pump the air into the balloon. It will take several pumps to inflate the balloon.

There is a tendency to overinflate a bal-

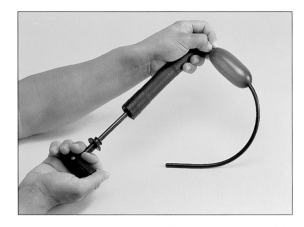

loon with a pump, so don't get too ambitious when pumping in air.

BURPING

Babies get burped after they are fed. But did you know that balloons also get burped? After you inflate a balloon to the desired length, let out just a "squeak" of air. This is burping the balloon. It is really important to do this, as it will soften the balloon and help prevent surprise poppings.

TYING A BALLOON

Now that you've managed to fill the balloon, here comes the challenge of securing the air inside. After you have blown up the balloon, let just little bit of air out to make the balloon soft. If the balloon is too firm, it

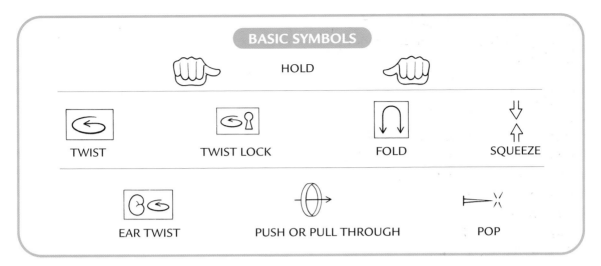

BASIC SYMBOLS

HOLD

TWIST

TWIST LOCK

FOLD

SQUEEZE

EAR TWIST

PUSH OR PULL THROUGH

POP

will be difficult to twist and it may even pop.

Wrap the mouth end of the balloon around your index and middle fingers. This creates a "ridge area." Use the index finger on your other hand to fold the mouth of the balloon through the ridge area. Pull it through and the balloon with snap shut.

BASIC TWISTS

Now that you have an inflated balloon, what can you do with it? You could hold it up proudly and tell your family you've made a snake. Or, you can twist and turn this colorful balloon and make something really amazing.

Strange as is might seem, there is a front part and a back part of a balloon. Always begin your twists at the mouth (knotted) end of the balloon. This allows the air forced out on each twist to move to the tail end of the balloon. If you have left enough space at the tail end, the balloon won't pop.

When twisting balloons make sure you always turn them in the same direction—i.e., all clockwise or all counterclockwise. If you change the direction of the turns, the bal-

loon will unravel and you'll be back where you started!

BASIC TWIST

The basic twist is the first thing you need to learn about balloon crafting.

1 Squeeze the balloon to the desired size.

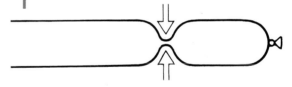

2 Use one hand to hold the end of the balloon while the other hand twists the balloon in three or more full rotations.

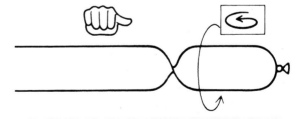

HINT: Hold on to both sides of the twist, or the balloon will unravel. Before you twist, decide on what size bubble you want to make.

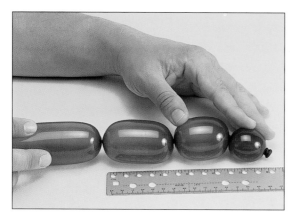

1 Make a small bubble followed by two medium bubbles. Remember to hold the first and last bubble or you'll be doing this again.

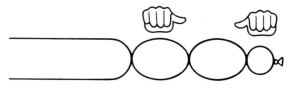

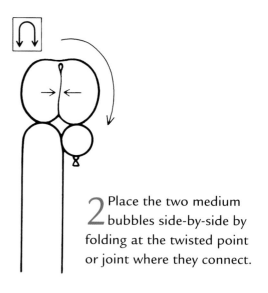

- A small balloon twist makes a bubble that is about 1 inch (2.5 cm) long.
- A medium balloon twist will make a bubble 1.5–2 inches (4–5 cm) long.
- A large balloon twist will make a bubble about 2–3 inches (5–7.5 cm) long.

When creating several balloon bubbles in a row, remember to hold on to the first and last balloon bubble. This isn't easy and may require either help from someone or the use of other parts of your body, such as your toes, knees, or elbows.

2 Place the two medium bubbles side-by-side by folding at the twisted point or joint where they connect.

TWIST LOCK

Now that you can blow up and twist a balloon, how do you get those bubbles to stay in place?

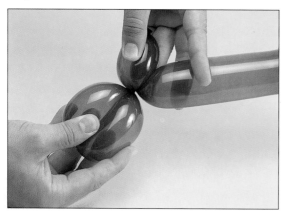

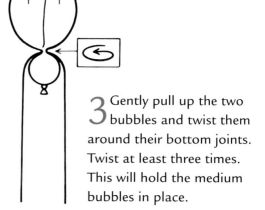

3 Gently pull up the two bubbles and twist them around their bottom joints. Twist at least three times. This will hold the medium bubbles in place.

EAR TWIST

This special twist is perfect for creating ears, a nose, or elbows on your balloon figure.

 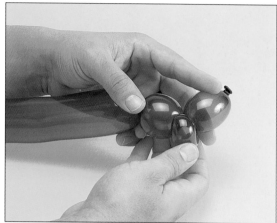

1 Make three bubbles: a small bubble, a smaller (less than 1 inch) bubble, and another small bubble the same size as the first one.

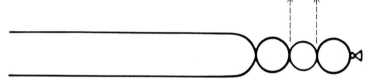

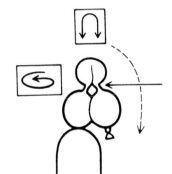

2 Pull up on the middle bubble at the joints while holding the two small bubbles together. Twist the middle bubble three times. This makes the tiny bubble into an elbow.

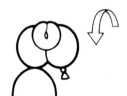

3 To turn this bubble into an ear, grab the bubble with your fingers and use your thumb to lay the bubble down on its side. You can also rotate this bubble to form a nose.

FOLD TWIST

A fold is the same as an ear twist, except that you use a large middle bubble instead of a small one.

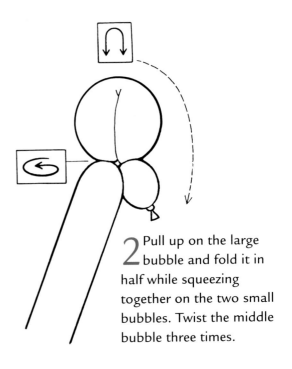

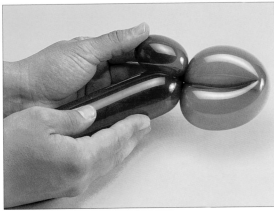

2 Pull up on the large bubble and fold it in half while squeezing together on the two small bubbles. Twist the middle bubble three times.

TULIP TWIST

This twist will take some practice. Use a clear balloon so that you can see the knot.

1 Twist a small bubble followed by a large bubble and then a small bubble the same size as the first.

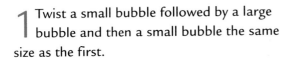

HINT: Pop-twist balloon creations are symmetrical. You have to twist the same number of bubbles for each side of a figure.

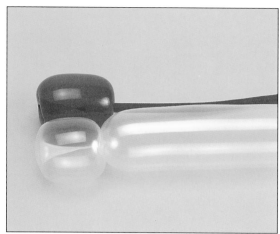

1 Hold a blown balloon several inches from the tied mouth end. Use the tip of your longest finger to push the knot into the balloon. Keep forcing the knot down until it is one or two knuckles inside the balloon.

2 With your free hand, grab hold of the knot and then pull your finger out of the balloon.

3 Pull up on the bulb of the "tulip" and twist the balloon. Make sure that the knot is below the twist with the remainder of the balloon.

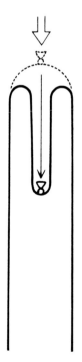
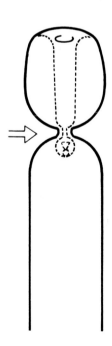
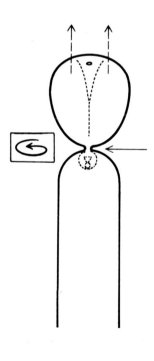

POP TWIST

What do you think will happen if a bubble pops while you are twisting a balloon? You'll be pleasantly surprised with this twist. When creating a pop twist, you generally need to make an uneven number of bubbles.

1 Make a medium bubble, then make a series of five small bubbles. Twist the first and last small bubbles together to form a ring of bubbles. The bubbles next to the pop-twist bubble are usually small bubbles.

2 Pull up on the second bubble and make an ear twist.

3 Do the same thing to bubble 4. This seals off the middle (pop-twist) bubble.

4 Use a pin to poke a hole in the middle bubble. If you have done your twisting correctly, bubbles 1, 2, 4, and 5 will still be inflated, but there will be two separate sides.

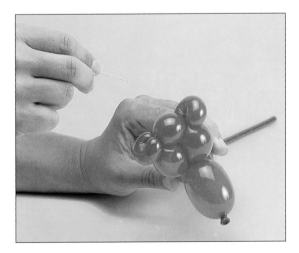

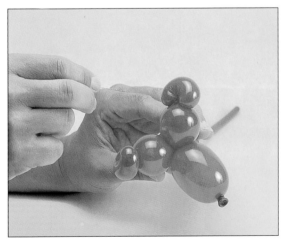

BALLOON PUFF

This puff seems to appear like magic at the end of a blown balloon. Do not try to do this technique by putting the tail in your mouth!

1 Pull the tail several times to loosen it. Then cup your hand around the inflated part of the balloon at where the tail begins.

2 Squeeze the air from the inflated section into the tail section. This will take a lot of practice.

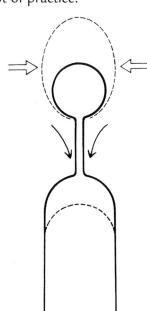

3 Adjust the size of the bubble by squeezing air from the puff section.

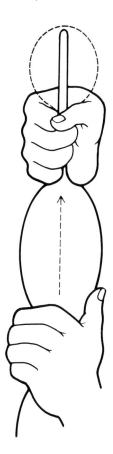

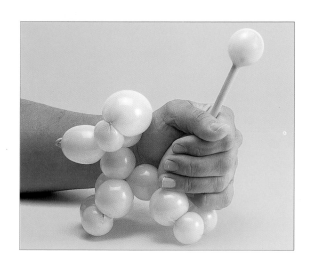

DIFFICULTY SCALE

Each project in the book is rated on a scale of 1–5. A 1 is the easiest, a 5 is the most difficult. This way, you may want to work on the easier projects before advancing to the more challenging ones.

Part Two
BALLOON CREATIONS

Chapter 4: Animals

Balloon animals, like real ones, have certain standard features. Each of our balloon figures will have a head, a neck, two ears, two legs, a body, two rear legs, and a tail. The twists are the same. Only the proportions will change. We will be using the 260, or animal entertainer, balloons for all of the animal projects.

DOG

There are a number of variations on the kinds of dogs you can make. By changing the amount of air in the balloon and the size of the bubbles, you can create different canines.

DIFFICULTY SCALE: 1

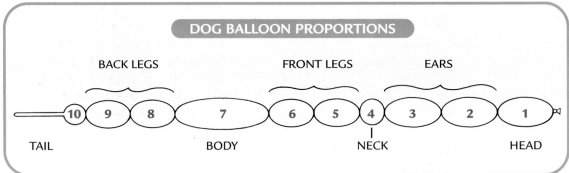

DOG BALLOON PROPORTIONS

BACK LEGS   FRONT LEGS   EARS

10   9   8   7   6   5   4   3   2   1

TAIL   BODY   NECK   HEAD

1 Inflate a balloon, leaving about 6 inches (15 cm) free at the tail. Twist a medium (2 inch, 5 cm) bubble. This is the head. Then twist two more medium bubbles. These are the ears. Twist lock bubbles 2 and 3 together. Your dog will now have a face and two ears.

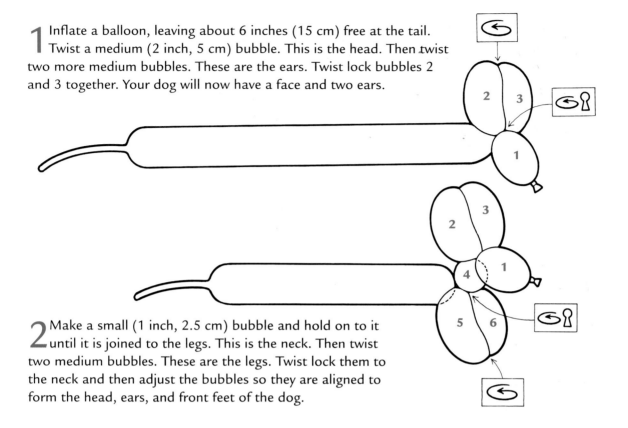

2 Make a small (1 inch, 2.5 cm) bubble and hold on to it until it is joined to the legs. This is the neck. Then twist two medium bubbles. These are the legs. Twist lock them to the neck and then adjust the bubbles so they are aligned to form the head, ears, and front feet of the dog.

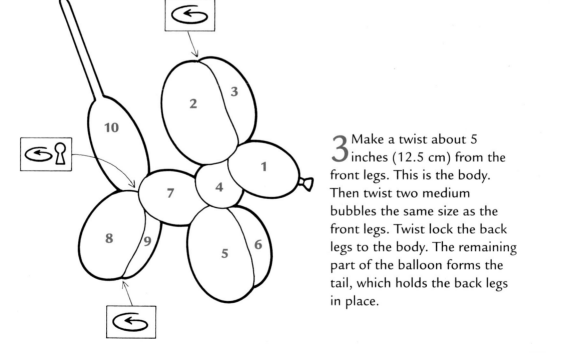

3 Make a twist about 5 inches (12.5 cm) from the front legs. This is the body. Then twist two medium bubbles the same size as the front legs. Twist lock the back legs to the body. The remaining part of the balloon forms the tail, which holds the back legs in place.

DACHSHUND

This dachshund is made the same way as our first dog, except for its ears.

DIFFICULTY SCALE: 1

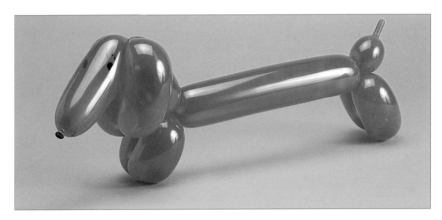

1 Inflate the balloon, leaving about 4 inches (10 cm) free at the tail. Twist a large bubble at the mouth end for the head. Twist two slightly smaller large bubbles for the ears and join them with a twist lock. Your dog will now have a face and two long ears.

Twist a medium bubble for the neck and two medium bubbles a little longer than the neck for the legs. Twist lock them to the neck. Adjust the bubbles so they align to form the head, ears, and front legs of the dog.

Make a twist about 5 inches (12.5 cm) from the front legs. Then create two medium bubbles that are the same size as the front legs. Make sure to leave a small amount of air after the last bubble. This will keep the legs from unraveling. Twist lock the back legs to the body.

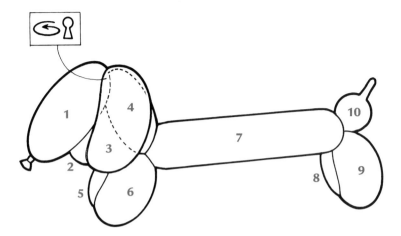

2 Now that you have made the dog, rotate the ears to point downwards. Use your fingers to pull the ears apart and tuck the head and neck in between them. Your dachshund is complete.

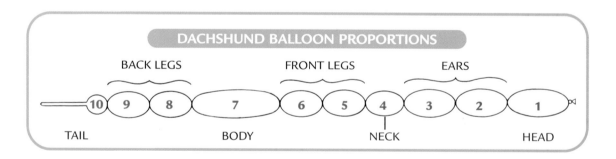

DACHSHUND BALLOON PROPORTIONS

BACK LEGS   FRONT LEGS   EARS

TAIL   BODY   NECK   HEAD

HORSE

DIFFICULTY SCALE: 4

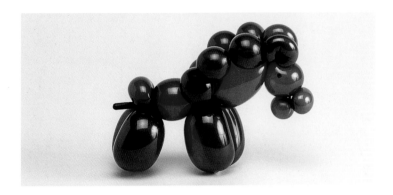

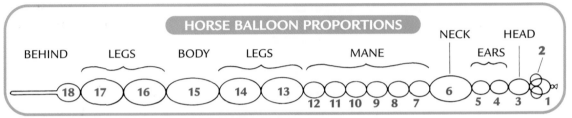

HORSE BALLOON PROPORTIONS						NECK	HEAD	
BEHIND	LEGS	BODY	LEGS	MANE			EARS	2
18 17	16	15	14	13	12 11 10 9 8 7	6	5 4 3	1

1 Inflate the balloon, leaving 6–8 inches (15–20 cm) free at the tail. Make a small bubble at the mouth end of the balloon. Then take the knot from the mouth of the balloon and wrap it around the joint of the small bubble.

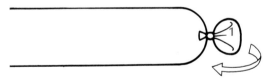

2 Pinch the small bubble in half and twist one of the halves three times to secure it. These are the horse's lips.

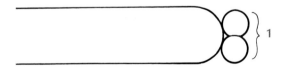

(HORSE continues on the following page)

3 Make one small bubble. This is the head. Make a smaller bubble. Lift it and do an ear twist to create one ear. Repeat to form the other ear.

Adjust the position of the ears so that the horse's entire head is in place.

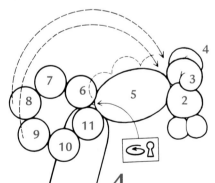

4 Twist a medium bubble to form the neck. Then twist six small bubbles to create the mane. Twist lock the first and last small bubbles together.

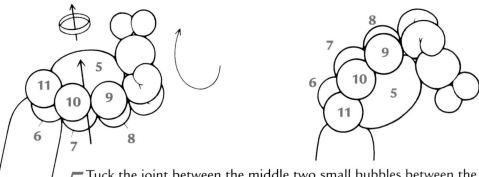

5 Tuck the joint between the middle two small bubbles between the neck and the head. Push the neck up through the ring of bubbles. Adjust the head and neck.

6 Make two medium bubbles and lock twist them together to form the front legs.

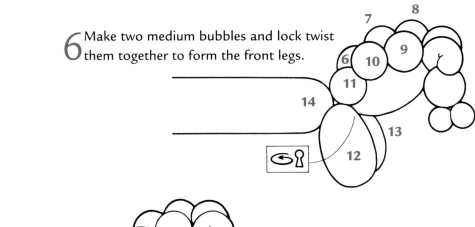

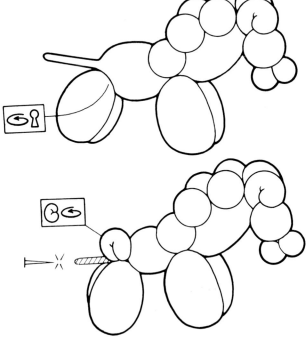

7 Make one medium bubble for the body. Make two more medium bubbles that are the same size as the front legs. Twist lock them to form the back legs.

Make a small bubble. Pull it up and ear twist it to make the horse's behind. Use a pin to pop the end of the balloon. This is the horse's tail. The last ear twist bubble should lock the air in so that the figure stays inflated.

PIG

DIFFICULTY
SCALE: 3

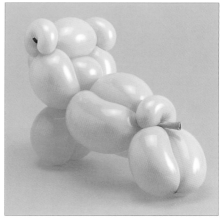

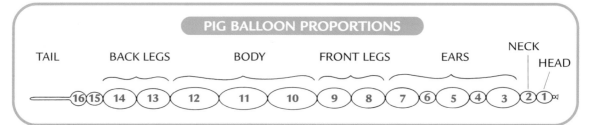

PIG BALLOON PROPORTIONS

TAIL	BACK LEGS	BODY	FRONT LEGS	EARS	NECK	HEAD

16 15 14 13 12 11 10 9 8 7 6 5 4 3 2 1

1 Inflate the balloon, leaving 8 inches (20 cm) free at the tail. Do a 1-inch (2.5-cm) tulip twist at the mouth end of the balloon. Twist a small bubble and hold it. Then twist five bubbles—medium, small, medium, small, medium— and twist lock the first and last bubbles together to form a circle.

2 Push the tulip bubble through the circle of bubbles.

3 Ear twist the small bubble on each side of the head. The head is now complete.

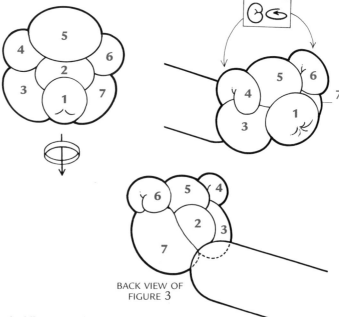

BACK VIEW OF
FIGURE 3

(PIG continues on the following page)

4 Make two medium bubbles for the front legs. Twist lock them together.

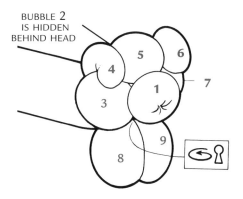

BUBBLE 2 IS HIDDEN BEHIND HEAD

5 For the body, make two large bubbles. Twist lock them together. Then make a third large bubble and push it through the two bubbles you just twist locked together. Rotate the body so that the third bubble is on top. This rotation locks the third bubble in place.

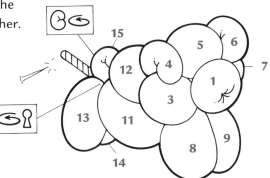

6 Make two medium bubbles for the back legs. Twist lock them together.

7 Make a small bubble and ear twist it. Use a pin to pop the end of the balloon. This gives you the pig's tail. If you wish, you can tie off this end to form a curl.

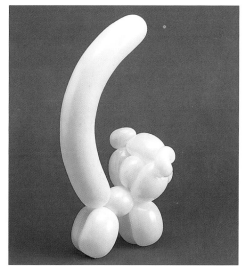

CAT

DIFFICULTY SCALE: 3

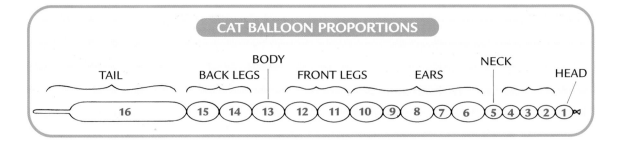

CAT BALLOON PROPORTIONS

TAIL | BACK LEGS | BODY | FRONT LEGS | EARS | NECK | HEAD

16 | 15 | 14 | 13 | 12 | 11 | 10 | 9 | 8 | 7 | 6 | 5 | 4 | 3 | 2 | 1

1 Inflate a balloon, leaving 6 inches (16 cm) free at the end. Create four small bubbles: one for the chin, one for the side of the mouth, one for the other side of the mouth, and one for the nose. Twist lock the second and third bubbles together. Then push the fourth bubble through them.

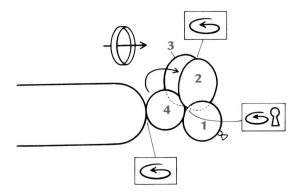

2 Make a small bubble for the back of the head. Then make five bubbles for the ring of the head—medium, small, small-to-medium size, small, and medium. Twist lock the two medium bubbles together.

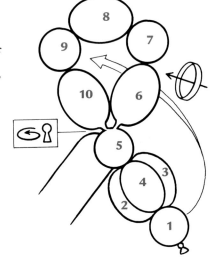

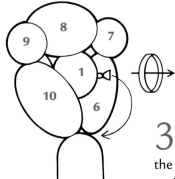

3 Take the knot at the mouth of the balloon. Pull it and the first four bubbles through the circle of bubbles. Then wrap the knot around the last joint of the balloon. The cat's nose and mouth are now in place.

(CAT continued)

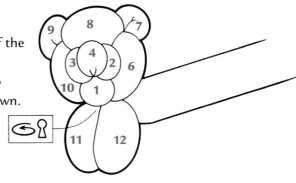

4 Ear twist the small bubbles on each side of the head. Instead of having the ears stand up, rotate them so that they lay flat on its side. To do this, turn and pull the ear-twist bubbles down.

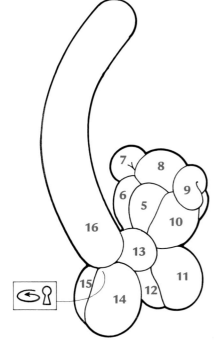

5 Make two medium bubbles for the front legs. Twist lock them together.

6 Make a medium bubble for the body, then two more medium bubbles for the back legs. Twist lock the back legs together. To complete the cat, grab the top of its long tail and roll it inward over your thumb. This will curl the tail.

Optional: Draw a face on the balloon using a felt pen with non-alcoholic ink, such as a Sharpie®.

TEDDY BEAR

DIFFICULTY
SCALE: 3

1 Inflate a balloon, leaving about 8 inches (20 cm) free at the tail. For the head, twist a medium bubble for the nose and a small bubble for the back of the head. Then twist five bubbles—medium, small, medium, small, medium—and twist lock them to form a circle. Push the first bubble (nose) through the opening. The second bubble (back of the head) tucks into the hole of the ring.

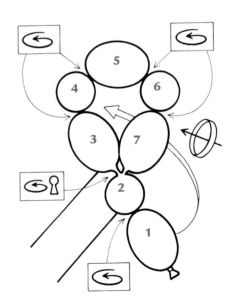

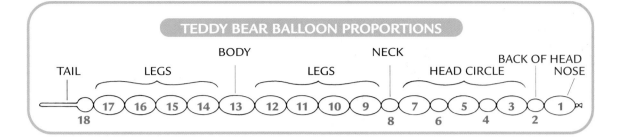

TEDDY BEAR BALLOON PROPORTIONS

| TAIL | LEGS | | BODY | | LEGS | | NECK | | HEAD CIRCLE | | BACK OF HEAD | NOSE |

2 Ear twist and lay flat the two small bubbles on either side of the head, as in
Figure 4 of the cat project. The head is complete. Make a small bubble for the neck.
Then make two small-to-medium size bubbles. Twist lock them together to make one
side of the teddy bear's front legs. Repeat to
create the other side. You now have the two
front legs of the bear.

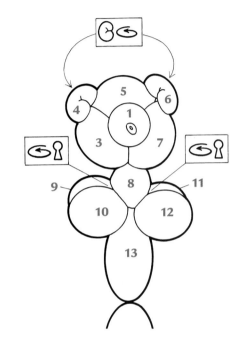

3 Make a medium bub-
ble for the body.
Repeat steps for Figure 2
to make the two back legs
of the bear. Be sure to
have enough balloon left
to form a little bubble
after the last joint. This is
the teddy bear's tail.

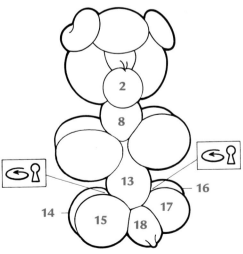

BUTTERFLY/DRAGONFLY

You'll need two balloons to create this figure—one for the body, one for the wings. It is preferable to use a different-colored balloon when making the wings.

DIFFICULTY SCALE: 3

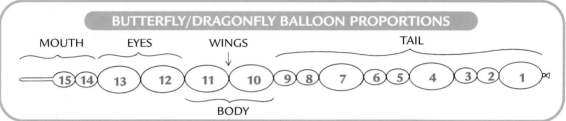

BUTTERFLY/DRAGONFLY BALLOON PROPORTIONS

MOUTH   EYES   WINGS   TAIL

15 14   13   12   11   10   9 8   7   6 5   4   3 2   1

BODY

Body:

1 Inflate a balloon, leaving 6–8 inches (15–20 cm) free at the tail end. Make a medium bubble. Make a small bubble and ear twist it. Make another small bubble and ear twist it. Align the ear twist bubbles with the medium bubble so that they lay flat. This is one section of the body. Repeat this step until you have made two or three sections. Adjust the bubbles after each section so that the body is straight.

Make two medium bubbles. Release the first medium balloon so that you will have a crease in the balloon. This is where you'll attach the wings.

For the eyes, make two medium bubbles and twist lock them together.

2 For the lips, make a small bubble and ear twist it. Repeat. Rotate the bubbles and adjust their position so that they look like lips. To create the tongue, use a small pin to poke a hole in the tail of the balloon. The ear twists will hold the air in the rest of the balloon.

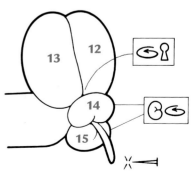

Wings:

3 Take a different-colored balloon and fully inflate it, leaving no free tail. Remember to burp the balloon before tying up the mouth. Squeeze the tail end of the balloon to create a .5-inch (1.5-cm) tail, then tie the tail and the knot (at the mouth end) together to create a balloon loop.

Bring the knotted end down so that it touches its opposite end in the loop. Twist the balloon at this point three times to create right and left wings.

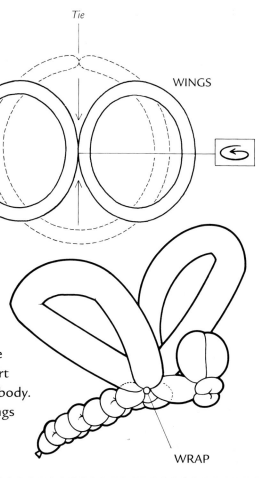

Tie

WINGS

Assembling:

4 Retwist the section of the butterfly's body at the crease to recreate two medium bubbles (see second paragraph of Figure 1 in body section). Insert the joint of where the butterfly's wings meet to the body. Twist it around the body three times. Adjust the wings and body into place.

WRAP

DRAGON

This is the ultimate Puff the Magic Dragon. It takes three balloons to make it.

DIFFICULTY SCALE: 5

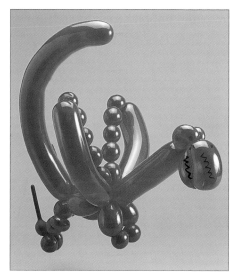

(DRAGON continues on the following page)

(DRAGON *continued*)

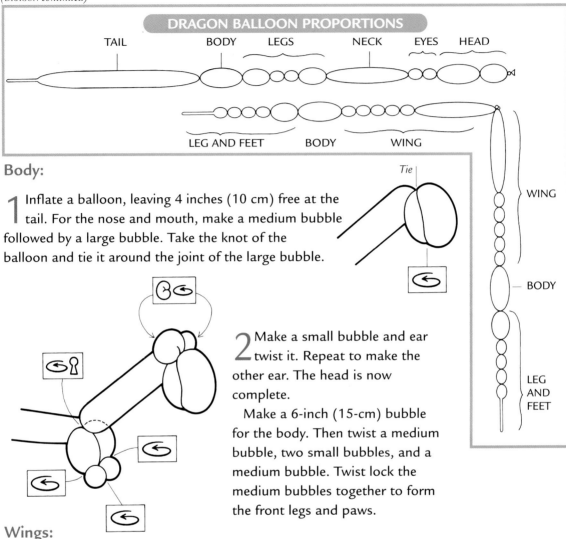

DRAGON BALLOON PROPORTIONS

TAIL   BODY   LEGS   NECK   EYES   HEAD

LEG AND FEET   BODY   WING

WING

BODY

LEG AND FEET

Body:

1 Inflate a balloon, leaving 4 inches (10 cm) free at the tail. For the nose and mouth, make a medium bubble followed by a large bubble. Take the knot of the balloon and tie it around the joint of the large bubble.

Tie

2 Make a small bubble and ear twist it. Repeat to make the other ear. The head is now complete.

Make a 6-inch (15-cm) bubble for the body. Then twist a medium bubble, two small bubbles, and a medium bubble. Twist lock the medium bubbles together to form the front legs and paws.

Wings:

3 Inflate two balloons, leaving 8 inches (20 cm) free at the tails. Place the balloons next to each other to make sure they are the same size. Tie the knots of the balloons together.

Choose one of the balloons and twist a 6–8-inch (15–20-cm) bubble from the knotted end. Then create five small bubbles. Twist lock the joint at the end of the fifth bubble with the knot where the two balloons are tied.

Repeat with the second balloon. You now have two finished wings.

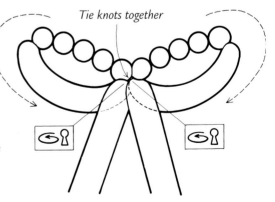

Tie knots together

Assembling:

4 Twist lock the joint of the wings to the joint of the dragon's legs. You will only need one good twist to keep the parts together.

Twist all three remaining balloons at about 3 inches (7.5 cm) down from the joint. Twist lock them together. If you have small hands, you can hold the balloon sculpture between your knees or have someone else hold the balloons while you do this.

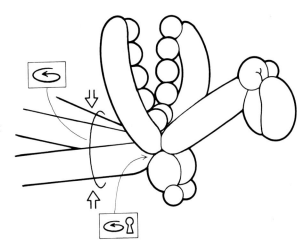

5 For the back legs, we will use the two balloons from the wings. Take one of the balloons and make a medium bubble, then a small bubble. Ear twist the small bubble to form the knee.

Make three small bubbles. Twist lock the second and third bubbles to form the foot.

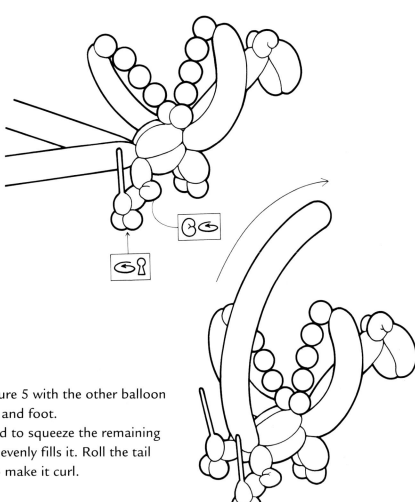

6 Repeat the steps in Figure 5 with the other balloon to form the other knee and foot.

For the tail, you may need to squeeze the remaining balloon to be sure that air evenly fills it. Roll the tail inward over your thumb to make it curl.

STEGOSAURUS

DIFFICULTY SCALE: 2

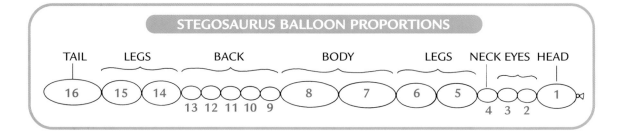

STEGOSAURUS BALLOON PROPORTIONS

TAIL	LEGS	BACK	BODY	LEGS	NECK	EYES	HEAD
16	15 14	13 12 11 10 9	8 7	6 5	4 3 2		1

1 Inflate a balloon, leaving 8 inches (20 cm) free at the tail. Make a medium bubble for the head. Make a small bubble and ear twist it for one ear. Repeat for the other ear.

Make a small bubble for the neck. Create two medium bubbles and twist lock them to form the front legs.

2 For the body, make two large bubbles. Twist lock them together.

Make five small bubbles for the spine. Open the body and loop the rest of the balloon down through and around the joint of the body. The joint between the last spine bubble and the rest of the balloon should lock between the joint of the two large bubbles.

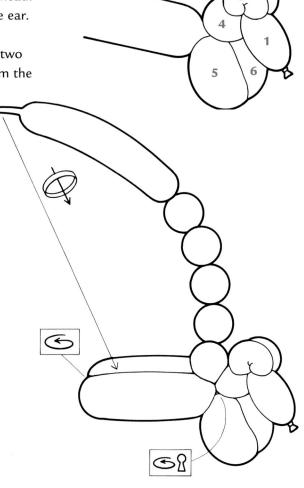

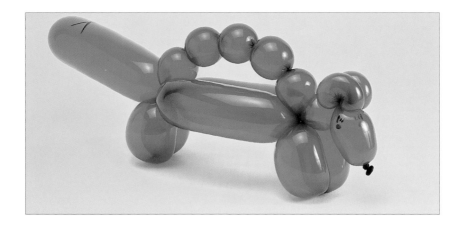

3 Make two medium bubbles for the back legs. They should be the same size as the front legs. Twist lock them in place. You should have a small tail left.

If there is enough room, make a small bubble towards the end of the balloon and ear twist it to create a spike. Or you can simply draw in some spikes.

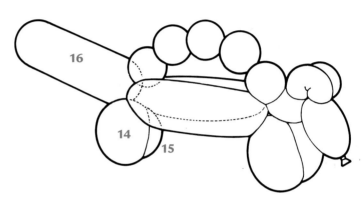

SCORPION

You'll need two 260 balloons to make this figure. And with a few variations, this scorpion can become a crab.

DIFFICULTY SCALE: 5

(SCORPION continues on the following page)

1 Inflate two balloons, leaving 8 inches (20 cm) free at the tail of each balloon. Place the balloons next to each other to be sure they match in size. For a claw, twist a small bubble and a medium bubble. Tie the knot around the joint of the medium bubble. Then make a small bubble and ear twist it. Repeat with the second balloon. You should have two identical claws.

Create a medium bubble on each balloon and twist lock the two bubbles together.

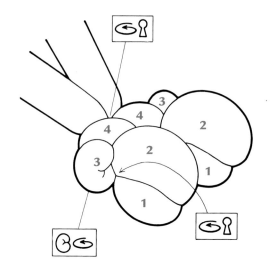

2 To make the legs on each balloon, make a medium bubble and then a small bubble. Ear twist the small bubble. Repeat.

Repeat the steps above on the other balloon.

Hold the remaining parts of the two balloons together. Twist them together at about 1 inch (2.5 cm) down from their joints. The remaining parts of the balloons may be different sizes. The longer balloon will be used for the body. The shorter will be the stinger.

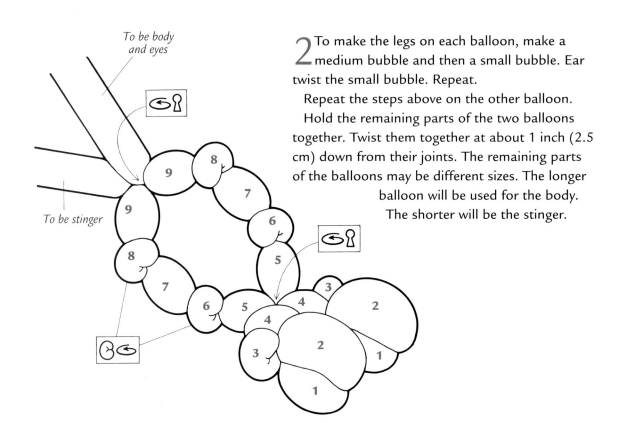

To be body and eyes

To be stinger

SCORPION BALLOON PROPORTIONS

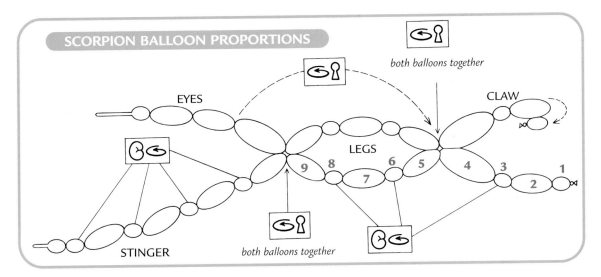

both balloons together

EYES

CLAW

LEGS

9 8 7 6 5 4 3 2 1

STINGER

both balloons together

3 To complete the body, take the longer balloon and bring it downward so that it rests on where the back of the claws meet. Twist a large balloon so that the joint of the large balloon is aligned with the point where the claws meet. Now twist the remaining part of the balloon and the claws together at this point.

To create the eyes, make two small bubbles and twist lock them together. Deflate the remaining part of the balloon with a pin and wrap it around the eyes.

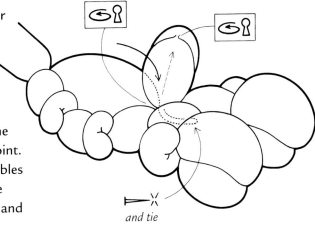

and tie

4 To make the stinger, take the shorter balloon made in Figure 2. Make two small bubbles and ear twist the second bubble. Repeat two times. This will cause the balloon to curl up like a scorpion's tail.

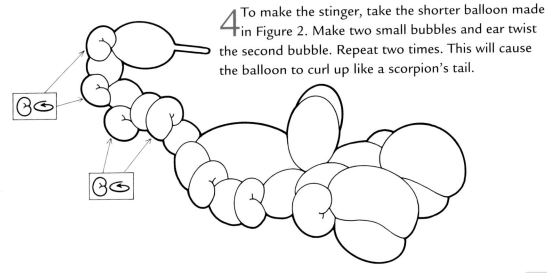

FISH

This fish requires one round balloon and one 260 balloon. You can fill the round balloon with helium and see your fish "float."

DIFFICULTY SCALE: 1

1 Blow up a round balloon. Then fully inflate the 260 balloon. Fold the 260 balloon in half and twist it at its center. Make a 1-inch (2.5-cm) bubble, then ear twist it. Repeat this on the other side of the center twist. These form the lips of the fish.

Wrap the 260 balloon around the round to help you with this.

Twist the two sections of the balloon together, but also include the knot of the round balloon in this twist. This will hold the fish's body inside the 260 balloon. If the body pops out while you are twisting the sections together, force the round balloon back between the 260 balloon once you're done. Bend the remainder of the 260 balloon to form the fins.

Option:

You can use helium for this project. Fill the round balloon with helium, but remember to anchor the balloon creation to a string so that it won't float away.

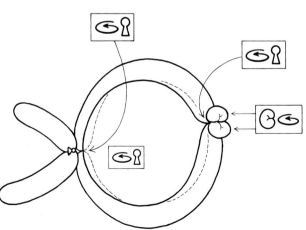

Fishing Pole

This fishing pole is made using a similar technique as the sword on page 79. Use two 260 balloons to make it.

DIFFICULTY SCALE: 2

1 Fully inflate a balloon and tie a knot at the tail end. Make a tulip twist at the mouth end of the balloon. Make a 4-inch bubble followed by an 8-inch bubble. Fold the 8-inch bubble in half and twist lock.

For the fishing line, use an unblown balloon. Tie one end to the knot at the tail of the fishing pole balloon. Insert the other end between the lips of the fish.

Make a 1-inch bubble and ear twist it. Your fishing pole is complete.

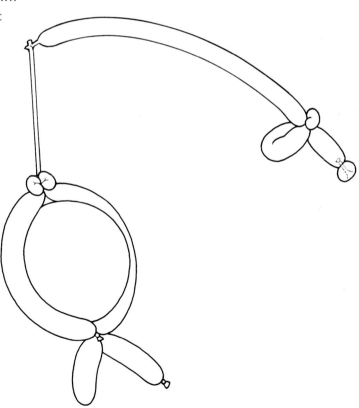

Chapter 5: Plant Life

Use animal entertainer or 260 balloons for all the projects in this chapter.

DAISY

This flower requires two balloons to make: a green one for the stem and a bright-colored one for the petals.

DIFFICULTY SCALE: 2

Stem:

1 Inflate a balloon, leaving 4 inches (10 cm) free at the tail.

Make a 10-inch (25-cm) bubble and twist. Add two medium bubbles and twist lock them together. This forms one leaf of the stem.

Repeat to form the other leaf of the stem.

Make a balloon puff at the tail end. Do not try to make a puff by putting the end of the balloon in your mouth. You could choke on the balloon.

Flower:

2 Fully inflate a balloon. Remember to burp the balloon before you tie it up. Squeeze the tail end of the balloon to create a .5-inch (1.5-cm) tail and then tie the two ends together. Twist the balloon at the point directly opposite the knot. The balloon will now be evenly divided into two parts.

Bring the two parts together. Place one of your hands about one-third of the way along the gathered balloons and twist. Then place your hands two-thirds of the way and twist. You should now have three equal sections.

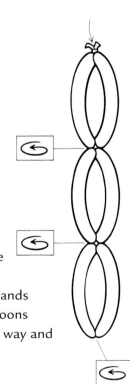

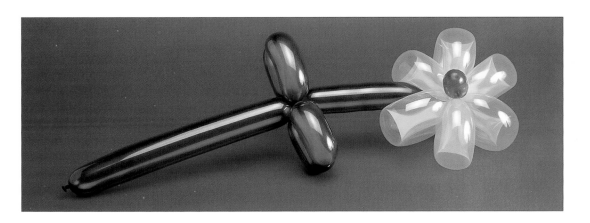

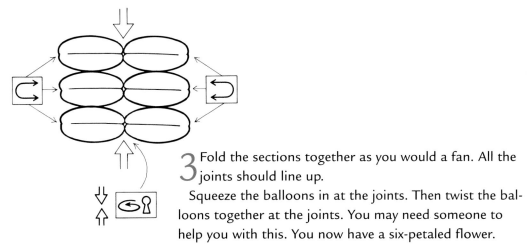

3 Fold the sections together as you would a fan. All the joints should line up.

Squeeze the balloons in at the joints. Then twist the balloons together at the joints. You may need someone to help you with this. You now have a six-petaled flower.

Assembling:

4 Hold the stem at the balloon puff. Fold the thin neck over and into the joints of the petals so that the puff stays in the center of the petals. You now have a daisy.

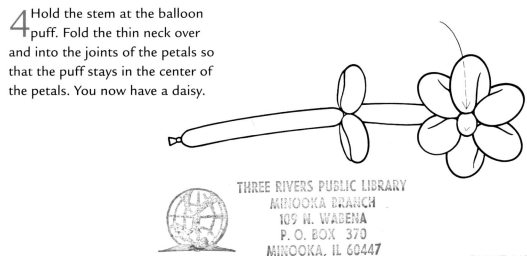

PALM TREE

You will need a brown and a green balloon for this figure.

DIFFICULTY SCALE: 2

Leaves:

1 Fully inflate the green balloon. Squeeze the tail end to create a .5-inch (1.5-cm) tail and then tie the two ends together. Twist the balloon at the point directly opposite the knot. It is now evenly divided into two bubbles. Bring the two bubbles together. Place your hands in the middle of the two bubbles and twist them together.

2 Fold over the two halves and squeeze them together at the joints. You now have four leaves.

3 On the underside of each leaf, divide the leaf in half and twist.

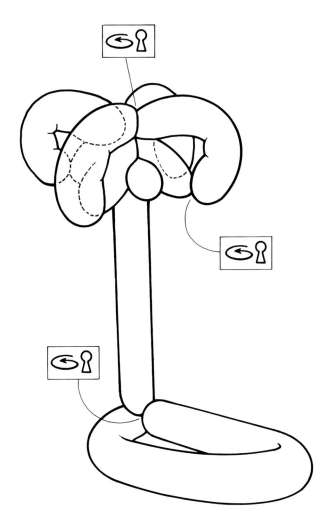

(PALM TREE continues on the following page)

Trunk:

4 Inflate the brown balloon, leaving about 1 inch (2.5 cm) free at the tail. Make a balloon puff at the tail end of the balloon.

Fold the neck of the balloon puff through the joints of the leaves so that the puff hangs down like a coconut. Make a small bubble at the mouth end of the trunk. Make a circle at the base of the trunk and twist lock the small tail bubble at where the circle closes. This makes an island for your palm tree.

TULIP

DIFFICULTY SCALE: 1

This project is basically the tulip twist technique (see pages 18–19).

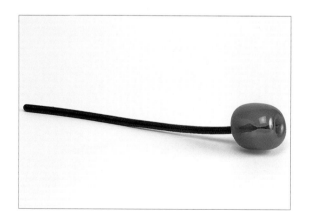

1 Blow a 2-inch (5-cm) bubble and tie off the balloon, leaving a long tail. Use your finger to push the knot into the balloon all the way to the end of the bubble and make a tulip twist. Then push the knot back up into the tulip.

Chapter 6: Other Fun Things

Now that you have mastered all the basic techniques, here are some other really interesting things you can make.

GUITAR

DIFFICULTY SCALE: 3

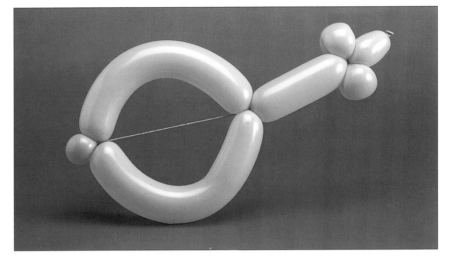

1 Inflate a balloon, leaving about 5 inches (15 cm) free at the tail. Hold your hands about 8 inches (20 cm) from the knot and fold the balloon into an S shape.

Gather the S together and twist the balloon in the middle of the three folds so that the folds stay together. Adjust the folds to make the head of the guitar.

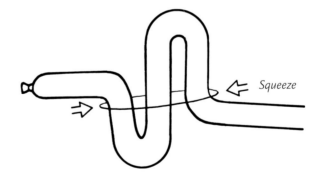

Squeeze

2 Make a small bubble where the tail begins. Holding the small bubble, make a circle with the balloon and twist lock the small bubble to where it closes. This is the body of the guitar.

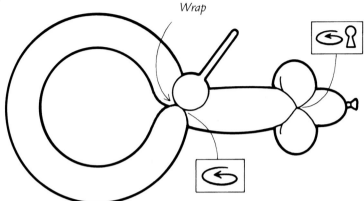

Wrap

3 Create a balloon puff at the very end of the tail. Squeeze all the air out of the small bubble into the balloon puff.

Twist the neck of the balloon puff about twenty-five times until it resembles a string.

Pull the string and balloon puff down across the body of the guitar and wrap them around the end of the balloon. Your guitar is complete. You can pluck the string to produce a twangy sound.

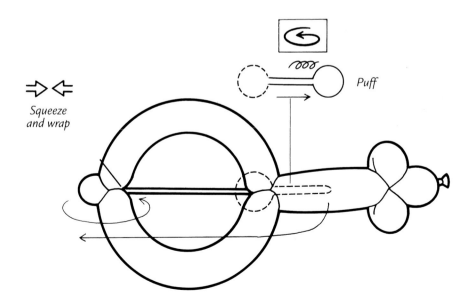

Squeeze and wrap

Puff

MOTORCYCLE

DIFFICULTY SCALE: 5

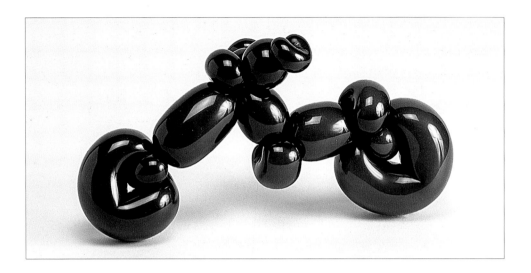

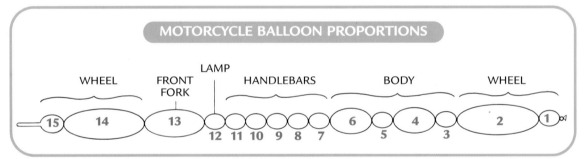

1 Inflate the balloon, leaving about 8 inches (20 cm) free at the tail. Make a small knot in the tail end of the balloon. You will now have a knot at both ends of your balloon.

Working from the mouth end of the balloon, make a small bubble. Pull the knot over the bubble and tie it around the joint.

Make a large bubble. Fold it in half, then twist lock the two halves together.

Fold the small bubble in between the large bubble. This makes the rear wheel.

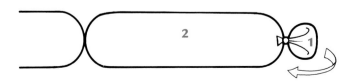

2 Make a small bubble and ear twist it.
This is the seat.

Make one medium bubble for the body of
the motorcycle. Make one small bubble and
ear twist it to create the engine.

Make one small-to-medium size bubble.
Then make five small bubbles. Twist lock the
first and last small bubbles.

Make a small bubble and ear twist it. This
makes the headlight.

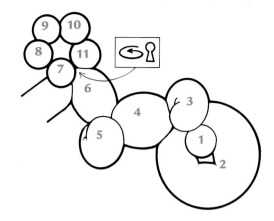

3 Ear twist the second and fourth small bubbles created in the
third paragraph of Figure 2. Then use a pin to pop the small
middle bubble. This will give you the handlebars of the motorcycle.

4 If necessary, give the leftover balloon a
good squeeze to move some of the air
down to the tail of the balloon. This will
make it easier to work with.

Make a small bubble at the knotted tail
end of the balloon. Then tie the knot over
the joint as you did in the second
paragraph of Figure 1.

Repeat the steps in Figure 1
to make the front wheel.

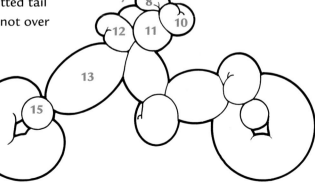

AIRPLANE

DIFFICULTY SCALE: 2

1 Inflate the balloon, leaving 7 inches (17.5 cm) free at the tail end. Make a tulip twist at the mouth of the balloon. This is the propeller of the plane.

Twist a medium bubble for the front of the plane. Make an 8-inch (20-cm) bubble. Fold it in half and twist lock the two halves together. Repeat. These are the wings.

Make a 3-inch (7.5-cm) bubble. This is the rear of the plane. Then make a small bubble and ear twist it. Repeat. Adjust the remainder of the balloon to stand between the ear twists.

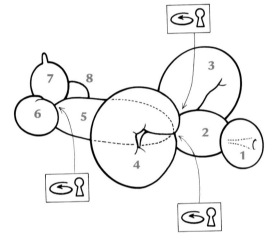

Optional:

Inflate another balloon, leaving about 1.5 inches (3.5 cm) free at the tail end. Attach the free tail to the front joint of the plane's wings so that you can fly it.

SPACESHIP

You will need two balloons to make this creation. White balloons make the best ship.

DIFFICULTY SCALE: 4

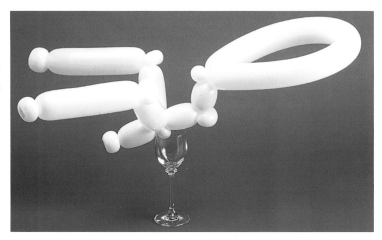

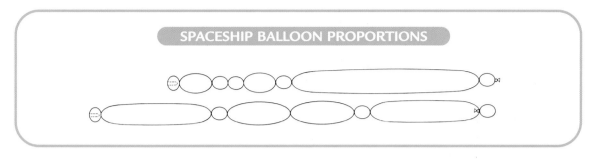

Front section:

1 Inflate the balloon, leaving 3 inches (7.5 cm) free at the tail end. Make a knot at the tail end.

Make a small bubble at the mouth end and fold up the balloon to create a 12-inch (30-cm) circle. Twist lock the small bubble to hold it in place, then twist the knot from the mouth around this joint.

Make a medium bubble and small bubble, then ear twist the small bubble. Repeat.

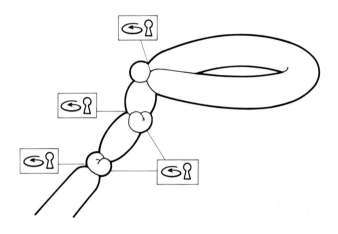

Back section:

2 Inflate another balloon, leaving 5 inches (12.5 cm) free at the end. Make a tulip twist at the mouth of the balloon.

Make a 7-inch (17.5-cm) bubble followed by a small bubble. Ear twist the small bubble.

Make two 4-inch (10-cm) bubbles. Let go of the first bubble to create a crease. Then make a small bubble and ear twist it.

Pinch the balloon tightly to create an 8-inch (20-cm) bubble. Don't let go. Poke a hole in the tail of the balloon and allow the balloon to deflate up to where you are pinching the balloon. Tie off the balloon, but do not let any of the air escape. Use a pair of scissors to cut off the excess latex.

Make a tulip twist at this end. Twist the balloon along the crease created in the third paragraph. You will have two halves of the spaceship's wings.

Tulip Twist

Tulip Twist

(SPACESHIP *continues on the following page*)

Assembling:

3 Bring the joint created in the last paragraph of Figure 2 to the joint of the second ear twist made in Figure 1. Twist the two balloons together at this meeting point.

Make a small balloon and ear twist it. Be sure that the ear twist ends up below the wings.

Make a 5-inch bubble. Then make a second bubble with a tulip twist at the tail end of the balloon. Then angle the wings of the balloons toward each other so that the finished creation looks like a famous TV spaceship.

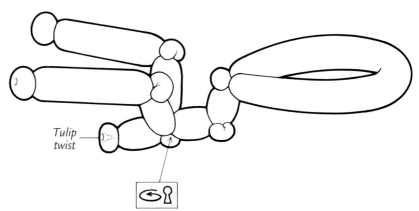

Tulip twist

SILLY BALLOON FIGURES

A sk for a latex glove, instead of a toy, the next time you visit the dentist. These gloves make a great novelty balloon.

DIFFICULTY SCALE: 1

1 Gather the opening of the glove together to form a mouth. Blow up the glove and tie off the opening. You might need an adult's assistance, as this can be tricky.

Use a marker to make a face. You can make the inflated glove look like a rooster, a spiky fish, or a silly person!

Part III
DECORATING WITH BALLOONS

Chapter 7: Chains and Braids

Instead of using crepe paper and masking tape, you can decorate a room with interesting balloon designs. A trick for keeping them up on the wall for a short time is to rub an inflated balloon against your hair. Your hair will stand on end and the balloon will stick to the wall.

Use the animal entertainer or 260 balloons for all the projects in this chapter.

SINGLE-CIRCLE CHAIN

DIFFICULTY SCALE: 1

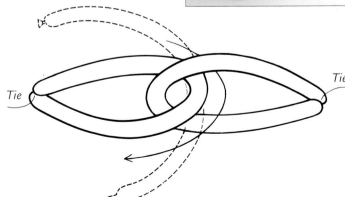

1 Fully inflate a balloon. Tie the knot to the tail of the balloon to make a circle.

Hang this circle on another fully inflated balloon. Tie the knot of the second balloon to its tail. Repeat until you have reached the desired length of chain.

FIGURE-EIGHT CHAIN

DIFFICULTY SCALE: 2

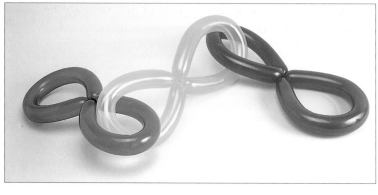

1 Fully inflate several balloons. Depending on how long you want the chain, you may wish to inflate ten or more balloons.

Tie the knot and tail of a balloon together. Bring the tied end of the balloon to its opposite end in the loop. Twist the balloon together at this point to form a figure eight. This is your first or anchor balloon.

2 Push an inflated balloon through one of the rings of the first balloon. Tie the knot of this balloon to its tail, then bring the sides together and twist to form another figure eight. Repeat until you have reached the desired chain length.

Tie

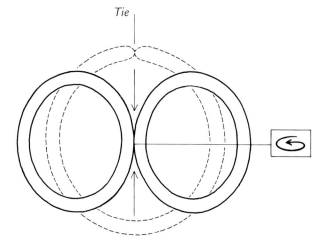

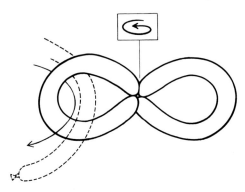

MULTICHAIN LINK

Color code the balloons for this project. It will make it easier when you are constructing the chain. It also helps to have the balloons inflated ahead of time.

DIFFICULTY SCALE: 4

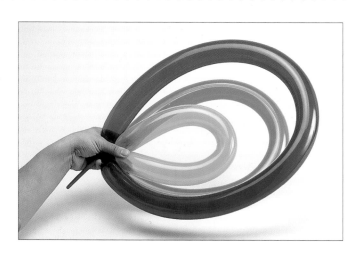

1 Fully inflate a balloon. Tie the knot and tail together. Inflate a second balloon to about three-fourths of the size of the first balloon. Tie the knot to the tail. Inflate a third balloon to about half the size of the first balloon. Tie the knot to the tail. You now have three circular balloons of varying sizes.

Using a string or uninflated balloon, tie all three balloons together at the knotted tops.

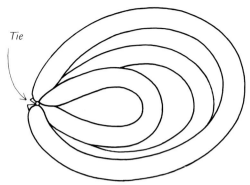

Tie

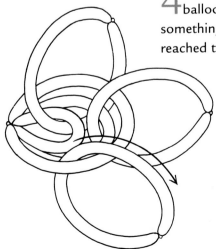

2 Thread a fully blown balloon through all three balloons, then tie its knot and tail together.

3 Thread another fully blown balloon through the middle and large balloons, but NOT through the small balloon. Tie its knot and tail together.

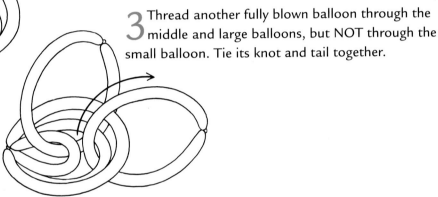

4 Thread another fully blown balloon through the three lowest balloons and tie off. You have a chain. Tie the top balloons to something high and continue making your chain until you have reached the desired length.

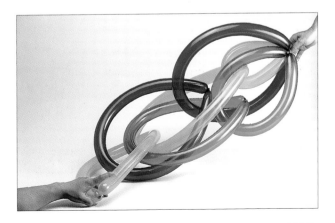

THREE-BALLOON BRAID

Use this braid to decorate a room, join the ends to make a gigantic hat, or join this braid with another three-balloon braid to make it longer.

DIFFICULTY SCALE: 2

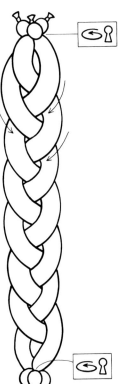

1 Fully inflate three balloons. Make small bubbles at the end of each balloon and twist lock them together.

2 Fold the balloons one over the other as if you were making a braid.

When you have reached the end of the balloons, make small bubbles at the ends of the balloons and twist lock them together to hold them in place.

Chapter 8: Special Occasions

Use animal entertainer or 260 balloons for all the projects in this chapter.

HALLOWEEN SPIDER AND WEB

DIFFICULTY SCALE: 4

Use white balloons for the web. Depending on its size, you should use about twenty fully-blown balloons. Use black balloons for the spider.

WEB

Inflate six balloons and twist their ends together to make the frame of the web.

Twist a balloon between the balloons of the frame. Continue in a spiral direction until the web is complete.

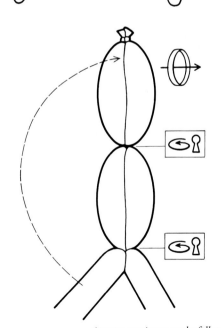

SPIDER

1 To make the legs, fully inflate four balloons and twist them together in the middle. On each leg twist an 8-inch (20-cm) bubble, then make a small bubble and ear twist it to make a knee.

2 To make the body of the spider, inflate two balloons, leaving 4 inches (10 cm) free at the end of each balloon. Tie the knots of these two balloons together.

Make a twist in each balloon about 8–10 inches (20–25 cm) down from the knots. Twist the bubbles together at this joint.

Fold these twist-locked bubbles over to measure out another pair of bubbles that will be the same size. Twist the second pair together.

Bring the two pairs of bubbles together and loop one of the loose ends of the remaining balloons through their opening to lock them together. This is the back half of the spider.

(SPIDER continues on the following page)

3 With the remaining ends, make a medium bubble on each balloon. Twist lock them together. This is the front half of the spider.

Make a small bubble and ear twist it for each balloon. These are the lips of the spider.

Fold down the remaining sections of each balloon to match the size of the bubbles made in the first paragraph of Figure 3.

Twist these sections together with the rest of the front half of the spider. The spider's body is now complete.

Use a pin to pop the remaining parts of the balloons. You can tie the latex ends around the joints to make sure your spider doesn't leak air. Use a pair of scissors to cut off the excess latex.

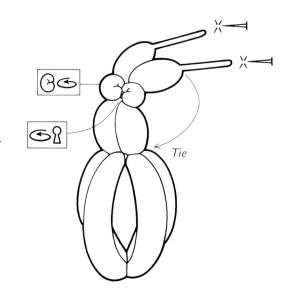

Tie

4 Twist the spider legs (at the middle joint) to the body at the joint between the front and back half of the spider. Adjust the legs so that four legs are on each side.

Tie

5 To make the eyes, inflate a white balloon to 5 inches (7.5 cm). Twist the balloon in the middle to make two equal-size bubbles. Place them side by side and tie the knot to the leftover tail. Cut off the excess tail. These are your eyes.

Separate the eyes and slide them over the lips.

Use a felt pen to draw on eyes. Attach the spider to the web.

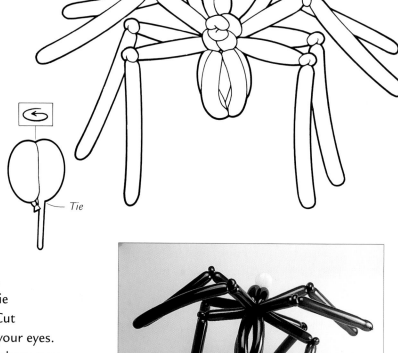

BIRTHDAY CENTERPIECE

You'll need three balloons for this centerpiece: two for the daisy flowers, one for the stem.

DIFFICULTY SCALE: 3

1 Make two daisy flowers (see pages 44–45, Figures 2 and 3). For the stem, tie a knot at the tail end of a balloon and fully inflate it. Make a tulip twist at each end of the balloon.

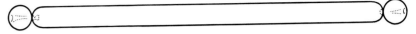

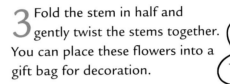

2 Thread a tulip bulb into the center of each daisy.

3 Fold the stem in half and gently twist the stems together. You can place these flowers into a gift bag for decoration.

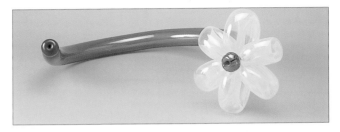

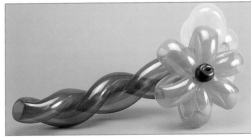

STARBUSH

This decoration can be hung from a ceiling or placed on the floor during a festivity.

DIFFICULTY SCALE: 1

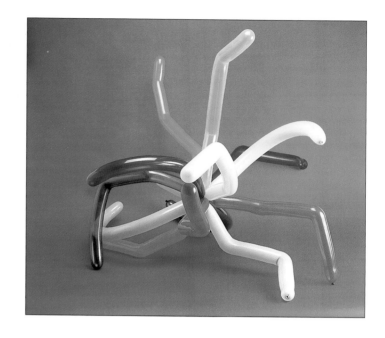

1 Fully inflate at least six balloons. Have an adult help you twist the balloons together in the middle.

2 Fold the balloons into different shapes.

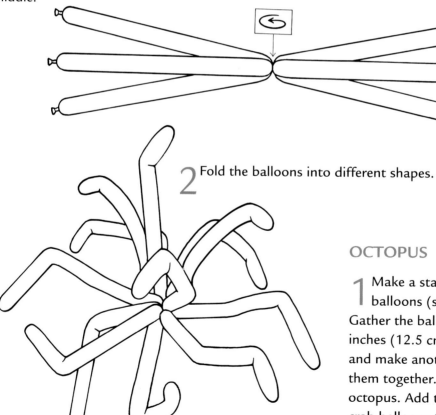

OCTOPUS

1 Make a starbush using four balloons (see Figure 1). Gather the balloons together 5 inches (12.5 cm) below the joint, and make another twist to join them together. Voilà! You have an octopus. Add this to your fish and crab balloons to create a sea life display.

Part IV
WEARABLE BALLOONS

Chapter 9: Bracelets

PLAIN BRACELET

DIFFICULTY SCALE: 2

1 Inflate about 8 inches (20 cm) of a balloon. Then make a medium bubble and a small bubble. Ear twist the small bubble. Repeat until you create the length of bracelet you want.

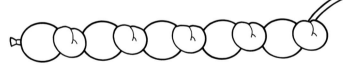

2 Tie the knot around the last ear twist joint. Use a pin to poke a hole in the tail end of the balloon. Tie the latex string around the joint of the last bubble. Cut off the excess latex.

Push your hand through the opening to wear it as a bracelet.

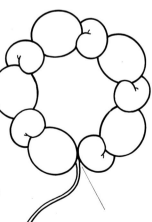

MOUSE BRACELET

DIFFICULTY SCALE: 3

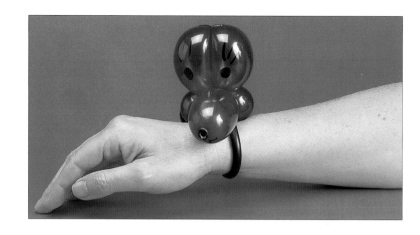

1 Inflate about 6–8 inches (15–20 cm) in a balloon. Make a small bubble followed by two medium bubbles. Twist lock the medium bubbles together. You now have the head.

2 Make four small bubbles. Twist lock the first and last bubbles together. These are the four legs. Adjust the remainder of the balloon so that it is positioned behind the mouse's head.

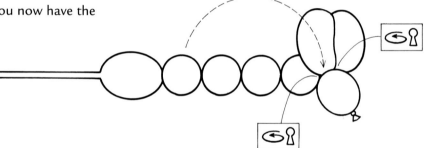

3 Pull the top bubble (the mouse's body) over the legs and wrap the tail of the balloon around the front and last legs several times. The tail should end up sticking out between the back legs. Your mouse is complete.

   To make a bracelet, take the tail out from the mouse's back legs and wrap it around your wrist. Then slip it up through the back legs again.

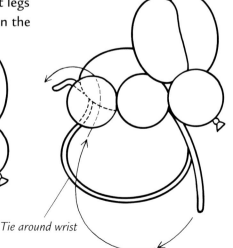

Tie around wrist

TURTLE BRACELET

DIFFICULTY SCALE: 3

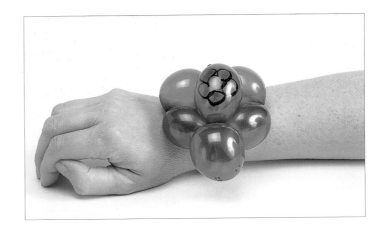

1 Inflate 5–6 inches (12.5–15 cm) of a green balloon. Make a tulip twist at the knot end of the balloon. Instead of pushing the knot into the center of the balloon, move your finger to one side of the inside wall of the balloon. Pinch the knot and twist the balloon. This will create a smiley face on the turtle.

2 Twist four small bubbles. Join the first and fourth bubbles with a twist lock. These are the legs.

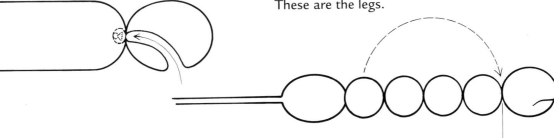

3 Fold the top bubble (the turtle's body) down and tie off the same way you did in the first paragraph of Figure 3 for the mouse bracelet. To create the wrist band, follow the second paragraph of Figure 3 for the mouse bracelet. Finish your turtle by using a marker to draw on the face and shell.

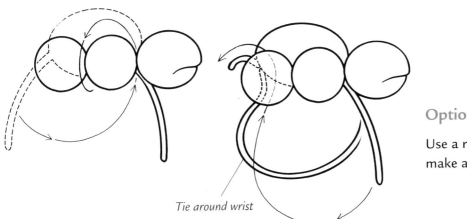

Tie around wrist

Optional:

Use a red balloon to make a ladybug.

Chapter 10: On Your Head

HAIR ORNAMENT

You will need two types of balloon to make this project: one bee body and one 260, or animal entertainer, balloon. With enough of these hair ornaments you can create your own headdress.

DIFFICULTY SCALE: 3

1 Inflate a bee body balloon about half full. Make a tulip twist by pushing the knot all the way to the beginning of the unblown portion of the balloon. Finish the twist.

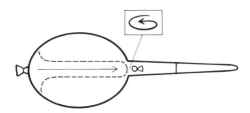

2 Push part of the uninflated section back into the balloon. The black tail should be poking out from the bottom of the balloon.

Twist the balloon in half to create two bubbles.

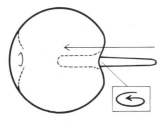

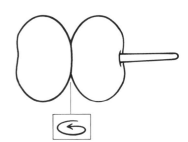

3 Inflate 4 inches (10 cm) of a 260, or animal entertainer, balloon. Using the balloon puff technique, inflate the tail end of a balloon until the bubbles at both ends of the balloon are equal size.

4 Slip the uninflated portion of the 260 balloon between the joint of the bee body balloon. Wrap it around the joint several times. Squeeze one end of the bee body. The bubbles will part like a hair-clip. Slide the open section onto your hair. When you let go of the balloon, it should lightly grasp your hair.

Optional:

You can wear this ornament as an earring.

TWO-BALLOON HEADBAND

U se different-colored balloons to create the most colorful headband.

DIFFICULTY SCALE: 1

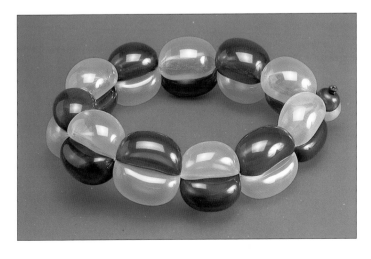

1 Inflate both balloons to about 18 inches (45 cm) and tie their knots together.

Starting from the knotted end, twist the two balloons together to form medium bubbles. Continue doing this until you are 2 inches (5 cm) from the uninflated section. You will have made at least nine pairs of bubbles.

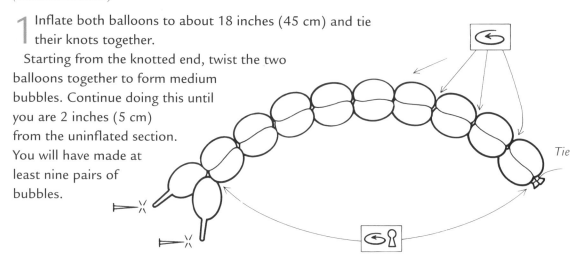

Tie

2 Twist lock the first and last joints of the balloons together. Then use a pin to poke a hole in each tail and wrap the tails around the last joint. Your headband is complete.

Deflate and tie

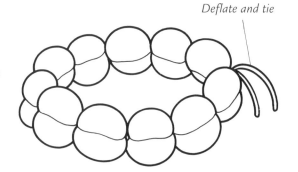

BASIC HAT FRAME

This frame can be used to create all kinds of silly headwear.

DIFFICULTY SCALE: 2

1 Fully inflate a balloon. Starting from the knotted end of the balloon, loosely wrap the balloon around your head (or a helper's head) to size it. Keep your hand on the spot where the knot touched the balloon.

Make a small bubble at the knotted end and twist the bubble to the section of the balloon marked off by your hand.

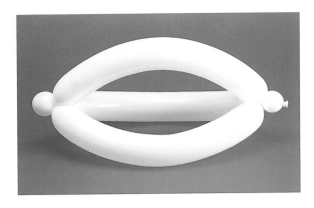

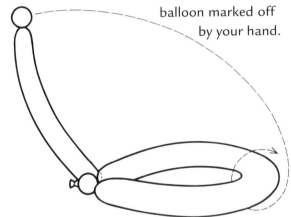

2 Make a small bubble at the tail end of the balloon. Fold over the balloon and wrap the bubble around the opposite end of the balloon. You now have the basic frame for hats. Use your imagination to make wild and crazy headgear.

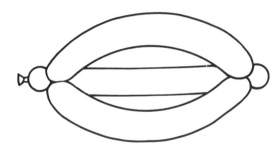

FOOLSCAP

You'll need four different-colored balloons to make this cap.

DIFFICULTY SCALE: 3

(FOOLSCAP continues on the following page)

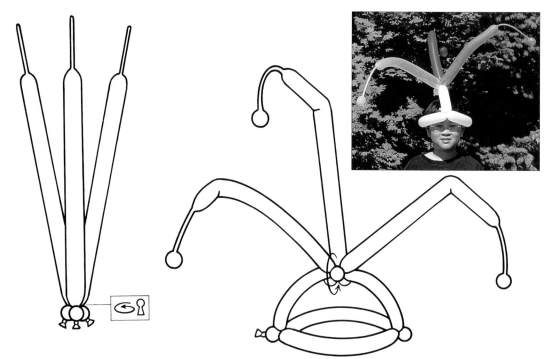

1 Make a basic hat frame (see page 69). Inflate the three remaining balloons, leaving about 8 inches (20 cm) at the tail end of each. Make a small bubble at the mouth end of each balloon and twist the three bubbles together to join the balloons.

2 Wrap the joined balloons to the middle of the folded-over section made in Figure 2 of the basic hat frame.

Using the balloon puff technique, inflate a bubble at the tail of each balloon. Then fold or curve the balloons into different shapes.

RING-TOSS HAT

Use two balloons to make this hat. You may want to make two hats in order to play ring toss.

DIFFICULTY SCALE: 2

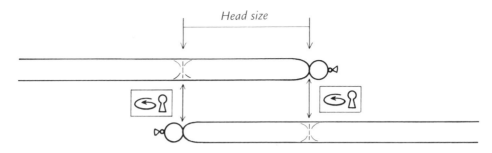

Head size

1 Fully inflate both balloons. Holding the balloons with the mouth ends pointing in opposite directions, measure the size of the person's head.

Make a small bubble at each mouth end and twist lock the bubble of each balloon to the correct point on the opposite balloon so that the hat will fit. This is the rim of the hat.

2 Gently wind the remaining parts of each balloon together. Do not twist so hard that the balloons form a joint.

When you have wound up to the tail of the balloons, twist lock the balloons together to keep them in place.

Repeat the steps for Figures 1 and 2 to make a second hat for a friend.

To play ring toss, fully inflate a balloon, leaving just a small tip on the tail free. Tie the knot to the tail to create a ring or circle. Take turns tossing the ring through the hat.

STARBURST HAT

You'll need five color-ful balloons for this hat.

DIFFICULTY SCALE: 2

1   Make a basic hat frame (see page 69, Figure 1), but do not fold over and attach the top of the balloon.

Fully inflate the four remaining balloons. Gather the balloons in their centers and twist. You may need an adult's assistance.

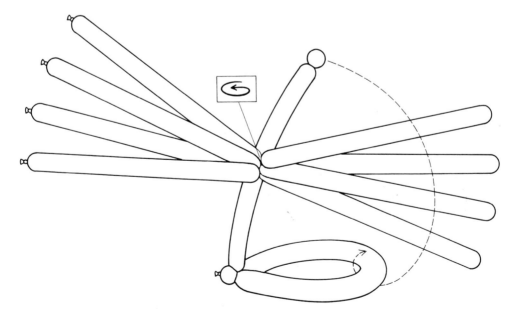

2 Twist the middle of the top of the hat frame section to the joint of the four balloons. Pull down the top of the hat frame. Make a small bubble and join it to the front rim of the hat.

Pull down the top of the hat frame. Make a small bubble and join it to the front rim of the hat.

Fold the starburst balloons into different shapes by creasing, bending, and folding the balloons.

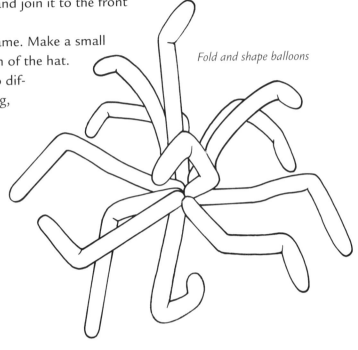

Fold and shape balloons

Chapter 11: Costumes

With a few balloons, you can make interesting costumes in minutes. Unless otherwise specified, use 260 balloons for all the projects.

BODY FRAME

DIFFICULTY SCALE: 2

This is the basic frame from which you can build on to make your costumes. You start with two balloons.

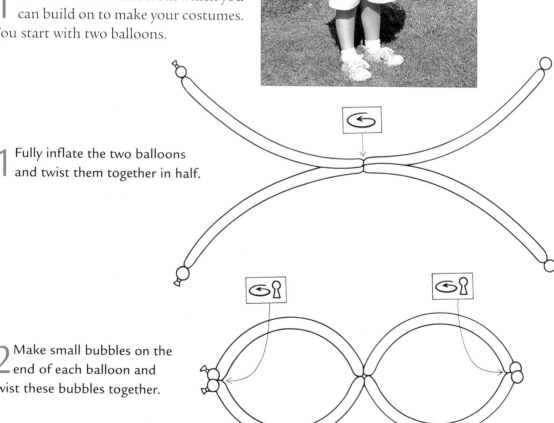

1 Fully inflate the two balloons and twist them together in half.

2 Make small bubbles on the end of each balloon and twist these bubbles together.

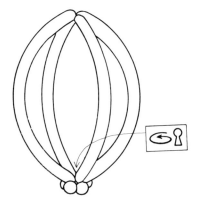

3 Twist all four bubbles together. Fit this frame on a child by slipping the balloons over the child's head and arms. The gathered end with the twisted bubbles is the back of the body frame.

BUTTERFLY

You'll need four balloons to make this costume: two balloons for the body frame, two balloons for the butterfly wings.

DIFFICULTY SCALE: 3

1 Build a body frame (see pages 74–75) and have a child wear it.

Fully inflate the other two balloons. Make small bubbles at both ends of each balloon and join the balloons together by twist locking the small bubbles. You should have one giant ring-shaped balloon.

Gather the twisted bubbles and twist lock them together. This will create two wings.

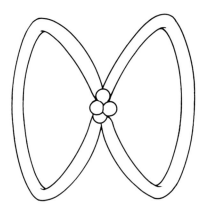

Twist lock the gathered bubbles of the wings to the gathered bubbles at the back of the body frame. Adjust the wings so that they hang correctly. You can fold the wings to give them a more triangular shape.

(BUTTERFLY *continues on the following page*)

Optional:

1 To make antennae for the costume, inflate two balloons, leaving about 8 inches (20 cm) free at the ends. Tie the knots of the balloons together.

Put the balloons around the child's head to size it. Then twist the two balloons together at the desired length.

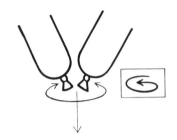

2 On each balloon, make a small bubble and ear twist it. This will make the antennae stand up.

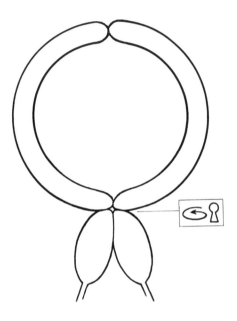

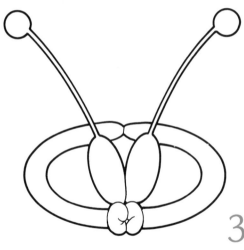

3 Using the balloon puff technique, inflate the tail end of each bubble.

BUMBLEBEE

The bumblebee costume is made the same way as the butterfly costume. But you'll also need a bee body and a 260, animal entertainer, balloon to make the stinger.

DIFFICULTY SCALE: 3

1 Make the basic body frame, wings, and antennae for the butterfly costume (see pages 75–76).
Fully inflate a bee body balloon up to the black tip.
Fully inflate a 260 balloon. Wrap it around the waist of the child. Twist lock the balloons together at the point where the balloon will comfortably fit.

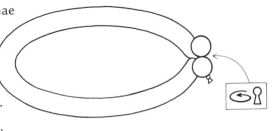

2 Make a medium bubble at the mouth end of the bee body balloon and twist lock it to the joint of the waist balloon. This forms a stinger for the bumblebee.

Optional:

To make the fairy costume below, make the butterfly costume (see pages 75–76). Then make the stem of a flower (see page 44) to form a wand.

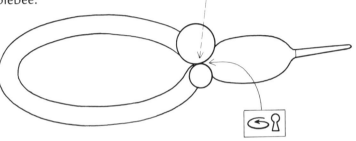

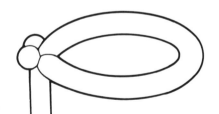

ANGEL COSTUME

DIFFICULTY SCALE: 4

1 Make the butterfly costume (see pages 75–76). Make a circle balloon and attach it to the four bubbles in the back of the body frame.

PIRATE WITH PARROT AND SWORD

DIFFICULTY SCALE: 3

Parrot

1 Inflate a balloon, leaving about 8 inches (20 cm) free at the tail. Make a small bubble, then a medium bubble. Fold the medium bubble over and tie them together with the knot at the mouth end of the balloon. This is the head.

   Make two 5-inch (12.5-cm) bubbles. Twist lock them together. These are the wings.

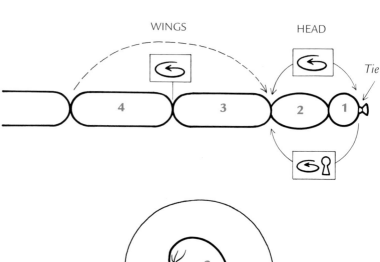

2 Make a small-to-medium size bubble (parrot's body). Wrap the joint at the end of this bubble around the twist between the two 5-inch bubbles. The head, body, and wings are now in place.

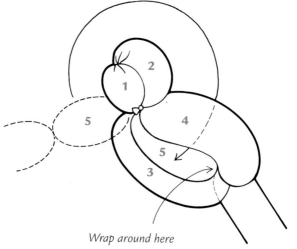

Wrap around here

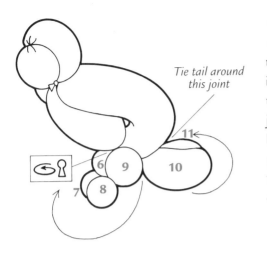

Tie tail around this joint

3 Make four bubbles: one medium, two small, and one medium. Twist lock the medium bubbles together. These are the legs. Twist the remaining inflated balloon into two equal-sized bubbles. Bring them together by tying the balloon's tail around the joint connecting the legs and wings. These are the back tail feathers. To hang the parrot on the pirate's shoulder, run an uninflated balloon through the legs of the parrot. Place the parrot on the shoulder and tie the balloon underneath the arm.

Sword

1 Inflate a balloon, leaving 3 inches (8 cm) free at the tail. Make a tulip twist at the mouth end of the balloon.

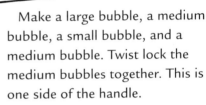

Make a large bubble, a medium bubble, a small bubble, and a medium bubble. Twist lock the medium bubbles together. This is one side of the handle.

Repeat the second paragraph for the second side of the handle.

Repeat the second paragraph again for the third side of the handle.

2 Ear twist each of the small bubbles in each side of the handle. Your sword is complete.

(PIRATE WITH PARROT AND SWORD continues on the following page)

Scabbard

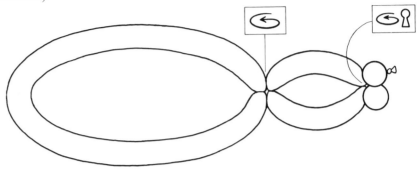

This is a fancier way of holding your sword.

1 Fully inflate a balloon. Wrap it around the child's waist. Twist the balloons together at the point where it fits comfortably. Try to have 7 inches (17.5 cm) remaining on both balloons. Make a small bubble at each end of the balloon and twist lock them together. This is the scabbard. Place the sword in it.

To complete the costume, add a basic hat frame (see page 69) and you're a pirate.

ROBOT

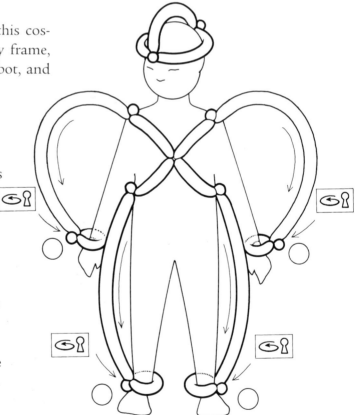

You will need eight balloons for this costume: two balloons for the body frame, five balloons for the parts of the robot, and one balloon for the hat frame.

DIFFICULTY SCALE: 4

Make the basic body frame (see pages 74–75).

1 Fully inflate five balloons. Make a small bubble at the mouth end of one of the balloons and attach it to the shoulder of the body frame.

Pull the tail end of the balloon down to the child's wrist. Make a small bubble at the tail end. Wrap the balloon around the child's wrist and attach the bubble to the balloon to keep the balloon around the wrist. Do the same thing with a second balloon on the other side of the child.

2 Make a small bubble at the mouth end of the third balloon. Twist the bubble onto the body frame under the armpit of the child.

   Pull the tail end of the balloon down to the child's ankle and attach the balloon as you did to the wrists. Do the same thing with the fourth balloon to complete the costume.

3 Make a basic hat frame (see page 69) and attach the last fully blown balloon from the back of the body frame to the top of the hat.

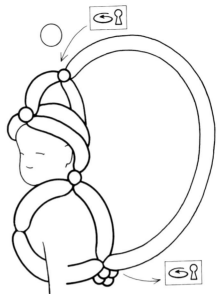

Chapter 12: Fun Houses

Balloons make great toys. They won't break windows, mirrors or other delicate objects. You can't poke your eye out or cut yourself with a balloon.

SIMPLE HOUSE

You will need a big room to fit this house, but it's worth the time and effort to make. Use seventeen 350 balloons.

DIFFICULTY SCALE: 3

1 Fully inflate all seventeen balloons. To make the base of your house, make a small bubble at the end of two balloons and twist lock them together. Continue connecting the ends this way with two more balloons until you have made a giant square.

Attach a balloon to each corner of your square by making small bubbles and twist locking them together. These will form your walls.

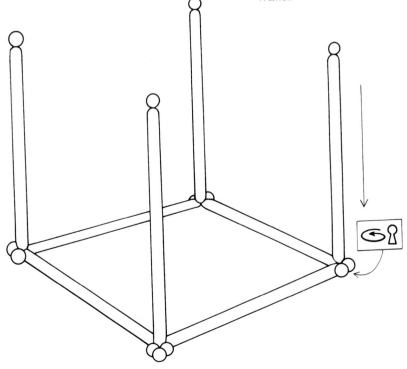

2 Use a balloon to join each of the bubbles of the wall, as you did in Figure 1.
To make the A-frame roof, add a balloon bubble to each of the four corners.
Gather two of the balloons from one
side of the house. Join them together at
the top and twist lock them using small
bubbles. You may need a tall person's
assistance for this step. Do the same thing
with the balloons on the other side of the
house. They will look like triangles.

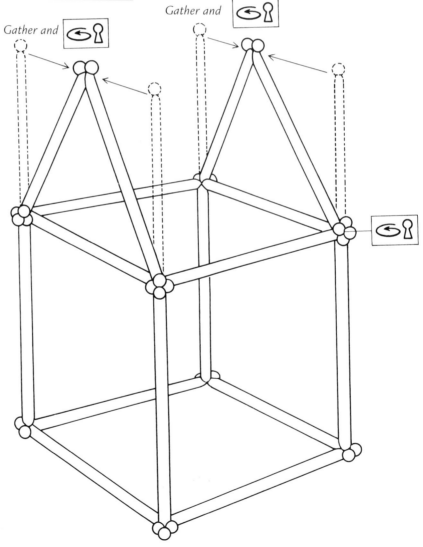

3 Attach the last balloon to the top of each A-frame roof.

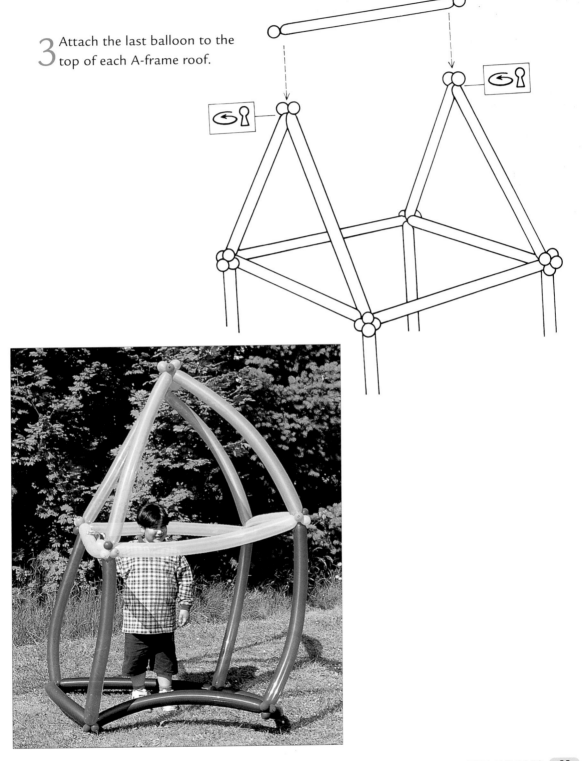

FANCY HOUSE

You will need a huge amount of space, like a big backyard or a large basement, to fit this house. You will also need lots of patience, plenty of air, and at least twenty-five airship, or 350 specialty, balloons. To assemble this house, use the same construction technique as you did for the simple house (see pages 82–85). You might want to fully inflate the balloons beforehand.

DIFFICULTY SCALE: 4

1 Using five balloons, make a small bubble at each end of the balloons and join them together. You'll get a pentagon, a five-sided shape. This is the base of the roof.

Attach the tail of a balloon to each of the corners of the pentagon by making a small bubble and twisting it on. Then gather these five balloons together and tie the knots at the top to create the roof.

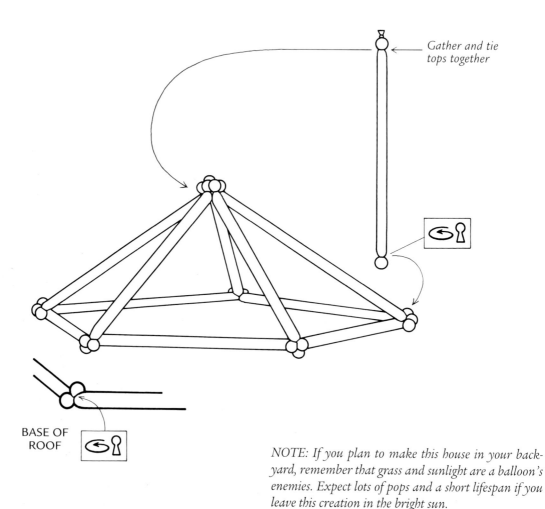

Gather and tie tops together

BASE OF ROOF

NOTE: If you plan to make this house in your backyard, remember that grass and sunlight are a balloon's enemies. Expect lots of pops and a short lifespan if you leave this creation in the bright sun.

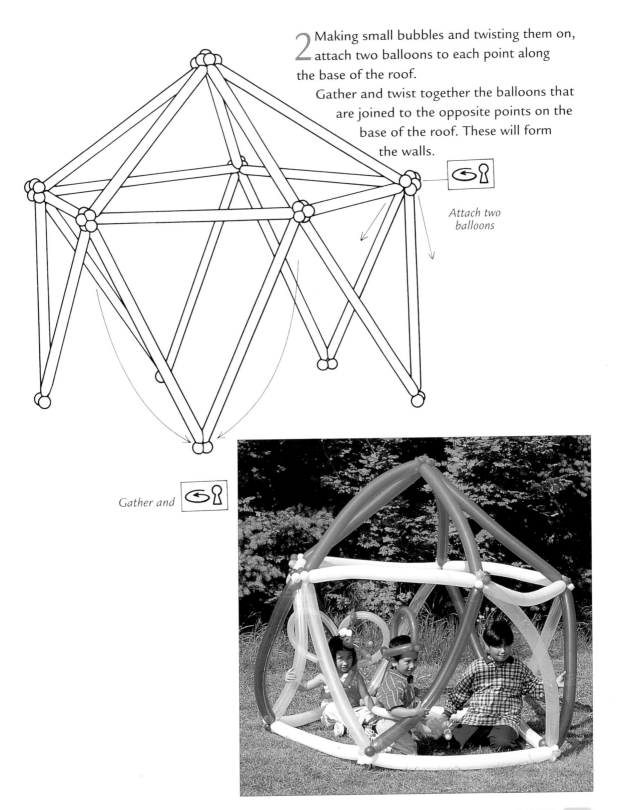

2 Making small bubbles and twisting them on, attach two balloons to each point along the base of the roof.

Gather and twist together the balloons that are joined to the opposite points on the base of the roof. These will form the walls.

Attach two balloons

Gather and

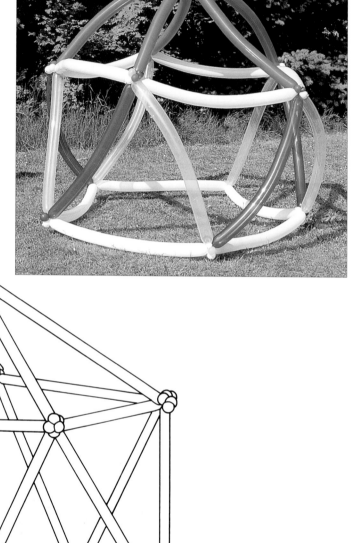

3 Add a base to the house by joining each of the walls to a fully inflated balloon. The house will be approximately 6 feet high (2 meters) and be 8–10 feet (2.5–3 meters) wide.

Attach base

Chapter 13: Games

BALLOON DARTS WITH BALLOON TARGET

You will need two 260, animal entertainer, or two 350, airship, balloons to play this game.

DIFFICULTY SCALE: 1

1 Fully inflate a balloon. Tie the knot of the balloon to the tail of the balloon. This is your target ring.

Fully inflate a second balloon. Stick two fingers in the balloon as if you were beginning to create a tulip twist. Hang on to the balloon by pressing your thumb against your two fingers inside the balloon.

Aim the balloon at your target and let go of the balloon. To make it more challenging, you can even hang the ring and try to shoot through it.

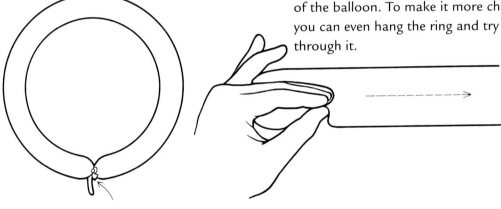

RING TOSS

DIFFICULTY SCALE: 3

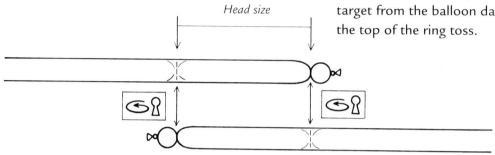

Head size

1 The ring toss is made the same way as the ring toss hat (see page 71, Figures 1 and 2). Instead of wearing the hat, use it as a game.

You can also attach your balloon target from the balloon dart game to the top of the ring toss.

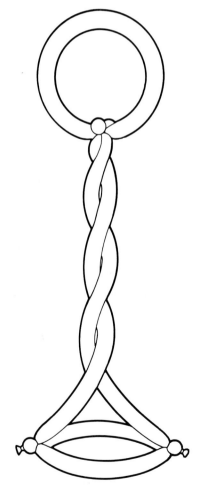

THREE-BRAID MAZE WITH RACING BALLOON BALLS

This creation will take loads of practice to make. You need three clear 260 or animal entertainer balloons for the maze and three 260 balloons in different colors for the three racing balls.

DIFFICULTY SCALE: 5

Racing Balloon Ball:

1 Inflate a 260 balloon. Make a small bubble (less than 1 inch) at the mouth end and twist it several times to be sure that the air is locked in. This bubble must be smaller than the width of the rest of the balloon.
  Push the bubble inside the balloon and grab it with your other hand.

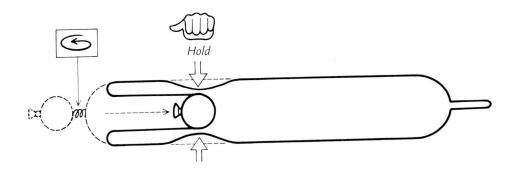

Hold

2 As you pull your finger out, twist it to the side to break the small bubble off the balloon. This will pop the end of the balloon but leave the bubble intact.

Twist and hook finger to the side when pulling out.

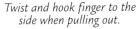

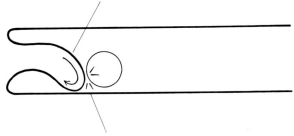

This will snap and cut the little balloon off.

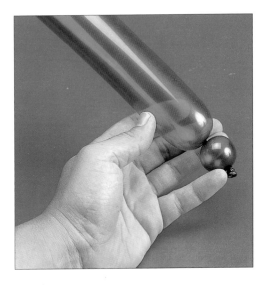

(RACING BALLOON BALL continues on the following page)

3 Use a pin to poke a hole in the tail. Cut off the excess latex using a pair of scissors. You should now have a tiny bubble. Make two more of these bubbles in different colors.

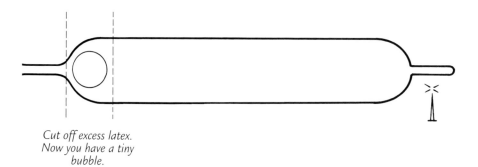

Cut off excess latex. Now you have a tiny bubble.

4 Fully inflate three clear 260 balloons. Take one of the small bubbles and push it deep into the mouth end of one of the clear balloons. Grab hold of the bubble.

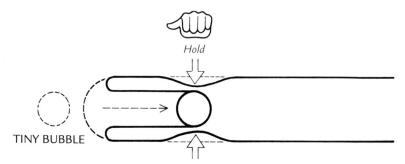

Hold

TINY BUBBLE

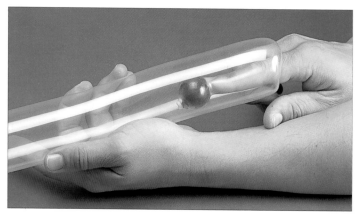

5 Using the same technique in Figure 2, twist your finger to pop the balloon. Remember to hold on tightly to the clear balloon, as you want to keep the air inside of it.

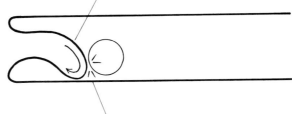

Twist and hook finger to the side when pulling out.

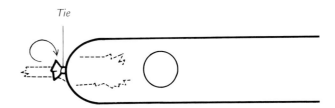

This will snap and cut the little balloon off.

6 Grab the mouth of the balloon and tie it off. If too much air has escaped from the balloon, blow more air into it and then tie. You will now have a colored bubble inside a clear balloon.

Repeat the steps for Figures 4–6 twice to make two more clear balloons with different-colored bubbles inside.

Tie

Three-Braid Maze

7 Braid the balloons together (see three-balloon braid, page 58). Then turn the balloon braid upside down and watch the bubbles race inside the balloons.

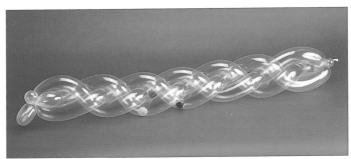

Index

ABOUT THE AUTHORS

Shar Levine is an internationally award-winning and best-selling author of hands-on children's science books. From 1987 to 1993, Shar created, owned, and operated Einstein's The Science Centre, a store that sells toys, games, and books in Vancouver, BC. In addition to writing books, newspaper, and magazine articles on science, business, and kids, she consults on the marketing and design of products and toys. With her writing partner, Leslie Johnstone, Shar has written the following books for Sterling: *The Microscope Book, The Optics Book, Fun with Your Microscope, The Magnets Book, Quick but Great Science Fair Projects, Shocking Science, The Science of Sound and Music,* and *The Bathtub Science Book.* Shar has also written for Sterling: *Awesome Yo-Yo Tricks* and *Marbles: A Player's Guide.* Shar lives in Vancouver with her husband and two children, Shira and Joshua. Besides being a writer, Shar is the president of a company specializing in portable tuberculosis isolation units and air purification systems. Go figure.

Michael Ouchi learned how to twist balloons while on the staff at the 1987 Edmonton Street Performers' Festival. He also learned how to juggle, do top hat tricks, and many other busking skills. Since then, he has performed at many festivals and special events in Alberta, British Columbia, Hawaii, Yukon Territories, and Washington State. Such highlights include: Calgary International Children's Festival, First Night Honolulu, and Yukon International Storytelling Festival. In 1996, "Tales from the Latex Skirt" debuted at the Yukon International Storytelling Festival. This was an interactive storytelling show where audience members and balloon creations became the characters in hilarious and amazing tales. Michael lives in North Vancouver with his wife, Tracy, and son, Maxwell. When he is not blowing up balloons, he is a computer software trainer and consultant. He says it's not much different from balloon storytelling. He puts on his costume (suit and tie), goes in front of an audience (his students), and tells them stories of bits and bytes.